More Grumpy in Spain

John Moody

Hope you enjoy the book

regards

John

x.

DEDICATION

To all those who want to write

To my old English teacher who said I had imagination, but my spelling would hold me back. PWEEEEW to you, eight books and counting, Honours Degree, and career in teaching. Who gives munchies if I can't spell Dyslexia, Oh! I just did.

To my cat that thinks sitting on my lap whilst I type is actually helping me. Most of this book was written with raised arms and wrists pointing down, a slightly cramp inducing posture for writing.

To anyone who feels like they would like to write a book, but don't think they are good enough.

JUST DO IT.

Many thanks to Judith for proof reading

The frustrated writer, extract from a writer friend

A bit over the top, but us creative types like to think we have to suffer for our art, it makes us feel more interesting.

Being creative is a hard cross to bear in life; it stops you holding down a regular boring job, and consigns you to freezing in a garret, whilst you paint your masterpiece, or endless hours, banned at the bottom of the garden, with your violin. In my case it was getting mild arthritis in my fingers from spending most nights pounding the computer keyboard. I missed out with finding girlfriends at the local disco, drunken nights with mates and later one divorce from emotional neglect, not that she ever listened to me anyway.

The big problem is that you cannot change; it is not possible to give up your instincts and do something sensible like becoming an Insurance salesman, or a bank clerk. We are doomed, unless we come (And I certainly don't) into that rare category that is called Genius, or just lucky to have sufficient talent to get published, your script taken up for a film, or a concert at the Royal Albert Hall.

My luck is to be in the 'not quite good enough section', along with millions of other hopefuls. My little pile of magazine articles, reside alongside my self-published fiction books and all piled on top of my computer, from which I type endless blogs for nameless promotional sites. So why do I keep going? Because, I love doing it. Creating something that did not exist before, even if nothing that I create is going to change the world.

"Spain offers such a wealth of intoxicating experiences for the mind, body and spirit (and not all out of a bottle!).

Contents

INTRODUCTION

Quite a few people commented that they wished the first book had been longer, but at that time I had run out of steam. However as they say 'pride comes before a fall,' the more I considered it, the more self-opinionated drivel came into my mind. The first book sold so well that I managed to get my car fixed. But the penthouse, executive jet, and gold Rolex will have to wait.

Most of the really interesting episodes (well they were for me) I have already described. So this book may contain less about Spain, and rather more about my opinions on just about anything. I think of it as going more global. However I have returned to some moments that more or less got left out of the first book, or elaborate on briefly mentioned episodes, when I remembered something that I had left out; the memory is not what it once was. But I decided why should I do all the work. I bet a lot of you have interesting, funny or even serious grumps about living over here. So, a few sections are devoted to those of you who supplied me with good material. I did reserve the right to re-configure the information to fit my style of writing and anonymity has been respected, but I kept as close as possible to the information supplied. There are some more of my drawings and some general information about this country that may be of interest, to those who may visit, or eventually settle here. Summing it all up this book may contain more stuffing than your great aunts old bolster.

The first Grumpy in Spain book was written in thirty days, because I had an internet boss cracking the whip and demanding 2,000 words a day. This one has no deadline, so I am going to have to be very tough on myself, if I want to finish it before I get too old. Often you cannot think about anything to write about, but the idea for the first grumpy book and now this one came from one line that I read by an internet writing guru, he said.

"Don't know what to write about? Bitch about life for 15 minutes"

Somehow by doing this every day I have managed to cobble together another book. The New Year is fast approaching as I write this so it's once again time for resolutions, by the time I finish this book it will be well into 2018, so we shall see if I can keep my new found enthusiasm. If you can't wait to find out, skip to the end of the book. I doubt you will miss much intelligent or enlightening literature in between.

I have now settled in Spain for almost 12 years. Despite any sarcastic humour that may raise its head in this book, I am genuinely grateful to a country that has allowed me to live the kind of life I always wanted , one that lets me breath.

I can't repay the understanding and generosity that I have received. To poke fun at the differences between nations, may not seem a very friendly way to reciprocate, but it is meant in a non-malicious way, and Spain certainly holds my heart.

Twenty years ago, I trudged to work in the rain at the local comprehensive school, mindful of ridiculous rules and regulations, homework and the prospect of 4G child thugs, reducing my classroom to chaos. If somebody had told me that I would, in a few years be living in a sunny country, living in a hobbit hole and writing, playing music and painting, whilst speaking to people in a foreign language, I would not have believed them. But here I am, and will be forever thankful to whatever fates conspired, because without a doubt, it has been the most exciting period of my life. I just wish I had come over when I was younger and fitter.

I have tried not to hang on to my old expectations; the last thing I want is to create a mini England in my home. The idea is to try and immerse myself in the feelings, attitudes, and complexity of my new chosen country. It's not easy to build connections and relationships with people, especially when there is a language barrier to overcome. But this country has so much to offer, and the more we become involved, the more that is revealed to us.

EARLY DAYS

Reading the first Grumpy book again I realised that I had skipped over many bits, so sorry, but this first chapter kind of backtracks, a bit like filling in the gaps, it also tends to jump from topic to topic. I could not think of any other way to fit them in.

I purchased my house in Spain on the internet. Nearly every place I looked at fell into certain categories. Overpriced ruins, new grey block apartments, and rows of villas that had been painted white, to try and make them attractive. Then there were fantasy cortijo's set in isolated splendour, and costing more than my home in England. Having warned many people to come over and look around first, I went ahead, and bought something on the strength of a description of Andalucía as the Garden of Eden. Plus a dozen photographs of a house, all of which looked really good. But they had omitted any of the views of the main road just outside the front door. How stupid was I? Very! Subsequent problems did not dampen my love of Spain, but they sure caused a few headaches, most of which were described in the first book.

Having to drive my few possessions down to Spain, I needed something slightly larger than what I had. I always fancied a Volvo estate, but any decent one was beyond my price range, until I opted for the bargain of the month, in fact it was free. Making ends meet before I set off, by doing a bit of private teaching of excluded difficult pupils, I was offered all sorts of things. One kid who was a known car thief promised to find me a decent Mercedes, I graciously declined his offer. His mate, who I also taught, said he could hot wire a car in thirty seconds. I pretended mild admiration, but told him that I did not want to be chased right across Europe by various assorted police forces. Another lad said I could have his dad's car, so I asked him if his dad would mind it suddenly missing. It turned out that his dad actually offered me it for free, because he thought I was a good teacher, and understood his son's problems with Authority. To an extent I probably did, but refrained from explaining that the so called authorities didn't give a damn about my opinions on mass education. Anyway I now had my slightly old, but apparently reliable Volvo estate. It eventually got me all the way, and ended its days high in the mountains, overlooking a wonderful vista, and is probably still there. The biggest problem on the drive down to Spain, in a car packed to the gunnels with ridiculous things, like beds and sofas, which I could have bought from Brits heading in the other direction, was that I had to do it one handed. Hoping to get a glimpse of my new intended Country from the deck of the ferry, I tried to haul myself up on to a higher platform and managed to tear some shoulder muscles. The pain was one thing, but for the next month or so, I could hardly raise my arm more than a few inches. Thank God a lot of the journey was on straight endless roads, because to change gear, I had to let go of the steering wheel with my good arm, and use that as quickly as I could before the car started to veer off the road. The same could not be said for two locals who had spent countless years driving the ten or so kilometres up the mountain road to the village that I lived in for my first three years in Spain. It had numerous bends and several fairly steep drops on one side. A week after the Council finally installed metal safety barriers; these two found one of the few gaps and promptly disappeared over the edge.

So I settled into my new life, and tried to integrate as well as I could. It was that, or be a recluse, as there was a distinct lack of other British in the area, although that quickly changed during the three years I lived there.

These villages are very fond of their traditions; most have a Saints Day where they parade the local effigy around the streets. My first village had San Lorenzo, who appeared to be carrying what looked like a giant toasting rack. In fact it kind of was, as it represented a torture implement, one that he was presumably stretched over at some point. Wonder if they gave him it as a memento after they had finished with him? At least he had a good book to read in his other hand. The reason I mention this figure is that I was commissioned to paint him as a large oil painting; it still hangs in the local bar next to the cigarette machine. That started the ball rolling, and I was being asked to do repeats at an alarming rate of knots. After about the fifth one it was definitely getting a bit boring, so I conceived a plan to sell raffle tickets, there would be just one painted each year, the money would go to the community, but I think the Council spent it on fireworks for the fiesta.

The local bar asked me to paint a large oil painting of their premises. I only accepted because they were going to pay me handsomely. Setting up my easel in the street I soon became the centre of interest in the village. The old guys who never had much to do but hang around the bar would stand staring at my painting and making informed (in their eyes) suggestions. They all wanted to be in it, sitting in their favoured positions. Whilst I was inside having a coffee, one slightly drunken old guy picked up my brush and painted an amateur looking cat in one of the windows, he and his mates were highly amused, until I wiped it out. I stuck it for two days, and then retreated to my studio with loads of photographs to finish the painting.

We had a local steep hill, or small mountain, depending on your point of view, if you had to climb it or not. At the top was a ruined castle of Moorish decent. I would often take the dogs and go up there, you could sit, eat your sandwiches and gaze down on the village far below whilst contemplating life. Each January 1st, a group of us would go up there to welcome the New Year. There is a funny story connected with it, although maybe not for those who were involved. When the Christians were taking Spain from the Moors, an army camped at the bottom of the hill and prepared to attack. The Commander of this Christian force decided to go off to Granada for instructions from his superiors, and told his men to wait for his return. As they greatly outnumbered the Moorish defenders, they decided to attack whilst he was away, I suppose to show initiative, or maybe they just drank too much whilst waiting. Anyway, they charged up the hill, but were so knackered by the time they got to the fort, that the Moors easily repelled them, and they had to stagger back down again. When the Commander returned he was so furious, that he had the ringleaders executed. Then he marched his troops up slowly, and massacred the Moors.

This area has its own micro climate, very different from a couple of hours up the road. People may know what snow is but they had not seen it in the village for over thirty years. It was such an event that everyone was outside taking pictures. Kids were having snowball fights and even the local street dogs were over excited. Parents were proudly telling their children that the last time it happened they were kids themselves. The local bar was full to overflowing in the evening, the whole atmosphere was like a fiesta, but by the next morning it had all gone.

I have mentioned in the previous book about Ben the metalworker who had his workroom in my cellar. It was quite a surprise to find out that I did not own everything. When I was bored I would wander down and stop him hammering on something, long enough for a cup of coffee and a chat. One day he was sipping a tea infusion. I asked him if he had grown tired of coffee, but he explained that he had toothache, and his mum had insisted that warm menthol tea with honey would ease the pain. I told him about English tea and how a builder could not survive for more than a couple of hours without a big mug full, and probably a lot of sugar. He said he had never tried it, so I promised to make a mug of tea with Yorkshire teabags and bring it down one day when he had recovered. When that day came, I presented a steaming mug of tea. He took it tentatively, sniffed it for a few moments, decided to take the bull by the horns and swallowed a big mouthful. Well actually, he didn't swallow it, but sprayed it all over the white wall. Using a few well known Spanish expletives, he declared it foul, and how could anyone like it. I explained that a whole nation was basically founded on it. He said he would not be visiting England in the near future.

The local bar, which was basically the only source of public entertainment in the village, had a host of characters that frequented it on a mostly permanent basis. Some drank copious amounts, but others seemed to need it as a place to hangout, both inside and outside in the street. It was a place that you could spend the whole day having a series of casual conversations and the odd argument, with a succession of people. Even when not in conversation, a lot of them were there just to eavesdrop on others, watch every movement and flow of traffic, and generally drift through another day. The bar opened early and shut late and some of the local men were there for all that time, day after day. The village was somewhat distant from any other areas of interest, so there were not even other options unless you just went home. Red Nose sat outside most days; he wore a large brimmed hat and generally sat there grinning. Corpulent and with a facial attachment that must have glowed in the dark, he watched the world go by. Leaving for the city early one morning, I passed him already sitting in his favourite spot, it must have been around 5am, and even the bar was not open for early workers. As I often saw him gone midnight in the same place, maybe he had been there all night.

Another guy could only speak in guttural croaks and gurgles. At some point he had obviously had a throat operation, judging by the permanent pad across his neck. He would hold quite animated conversations with the other locals, who seemed, or at least pretended to understand him. Most of the time he was ok, but when angry he would stomp around giving Hitler salutes and gesticulating with his pen knife, indicating what he would do to anyone who got in his way. He lived on the edge of the village in a rundown set of buildings, protected by barbed wire. He served a bit of time for attacking his ex-wife with the same penknife. Last time I revisited the village, I was told he had died, like a surprising number of them from the bar.

One of the funniest sights was seeing all the old guys, with their glasses misted up, watching a troop of Amazonian semi naked African female dancers, who came to perform at the Annual fiesta. The average height of the local men was about five foot six, whereas the average height of these women was more like six foot. They were certainly very well endowed and sexy. Gyrating around the tables, and at times snuggling up behind the odd guy or two. You could see in the faces of the men that they had never experienced such up front (so to speak) action before. The local women looked on with mild amusement, seeing their menfolk looking all hot and flustered. When the dance troop moved on to the next bar, most of the blokes scuttled off down side alleys to get there before them. There was one male dancer, shiny black and rippling muscles, so some of the women also scuttled after him. When the local organisers met to arrange the next years events it was not surprising that they were invited back.

I have a friend who looks a bit like a Rastafarian, although he is not adverse to wearing interesting clothes such as pink leather jackets. The people in this mountain village were not unaware of the black guys down on the coast, but up here there were none and certainly none with the flair of my friend. He was visiting after doing a course of salsa dancing in Madrid. When we entered the local bar all suspicious eyes were on him, but being an extrovert, within half an hour, he was up and dancing in the middle of the bar, teaching them salsa and being joined by one or two of the locals.

The village was perched on a steep slope, the old part full of rambling alleyways between whitewashed small homes all cramped together, was difficult to walk down even for able bodied people. The alleyways were often rough cobbles, cracked or subsided slabs with water runnels down their centre. It was definitely like going back in time. You would in places have to duck under washing stretched across the alley, many doors had old bottles of water tied to them, or placed on the step. Apparently flies saw their reflection much magnified in them and would bugger off rather than enter the open doorways. The odd snarling dog protecting its territory, and loads of wild cats would scatter in all directions hissing at you. It didn't seem to matter if somebody piled a load of sand or bricks in the way, normally there was always an adjacent alley. Some of the more open roads down into it tempted motorists to descend, till they were trapped in a gradually thinning path, or even a sudden set of steps. One driver managed to wedge their car between two houses, much to the amusement of the locals. Some residents who had years of experience, could manage to get their vehicles around impossibly tight bends, rather than park and walk to their homes. Anyway this paragraph was meant to be about this old guy, who would walk up from the lower reaches of the village to the Pharmacia which was up near my home on the high ground. It would take him most of the morning at a snail's pace. I was in there one day when he called in for his prescription. A temporary assistant would not give him it, because he did not have the right paperwork, which he had left at home. Rather than argue, he simply smiled and said he would get it. With that he turned around and left. A good couple of hours later I saw him pass my house on his return to the chemist with the right paper. In all he must have walked for over five hours before he eventually got home. I don't suppose he had much else to do, and time is very different for a lot of the older people in these villages, they don't like rushing. I did offer to go and get his paperwork, the alleyways prevented me using my car to take him, but I would have walked it quick enough, whilst he had a coffee or two in the bar. But he politely and very gently refused, saying the exercise would do him good. I wish at times I could be as calm and accepting as him, especially when faced by petty officialdom.

Many of the locals had spent their whole lives in the village, rarely leaving it. My old neighbour would often regale me with the same story about the time she had been whisked away to Granada by a relative, who at the age of 45 had just bought his first car. She explained in great detail how the shops were so big, and she had never seen so many people in one place. I did not have the heart to say that I had already been there twice that week.

In the past the majority of marriages took place between neighbours, or at least somebody from a nearby village. I was told by another ancient neighbour, that when she was young, they would walk down to Motril for the weekend dance. In a car, on the new road it would take me about forty minutes. On an old track it took them several hours, including at one point travelling along a river bed. They would dance until the early hours, then as a group of youngsters walk all the way back, arriving well into Sunday morning.

The local old ladies loved nothing better than spreading rumours. I lived on my own, so for some reason they got it into their heads that I must be gay, because I did my own washing, and hung my wet underwear to dry on my balcony. I also cooked my own meals, something that was definitely rare amongst the males of the village. They were not backward in coming forward, and even asked me outright. I wasn't, and I pointed out that if I was, where was my boyfriend ? This being cleared up, they obviously had a meeting and decided they would find me a girlfriend. On average every couple of weeks one old lady or another would call bringing with her some middle aged relative who had always been single, or whose husband had vanished, or even one of them that was still wearing all black. We would sit on facing seats sipping coffee and smiling politely at each other, whilst the old lady would rattle on about the latest suitors attributes. I don't think I have ever felt so embarrassed, surpassing even the time I farted loudly whilst nervously presenting the local mayor with a painting. These women did not seem to be at all phased by the fact that someone was describing how big and warm they would be on a cold night, (honest) or how they would be just what a lonely man needed. Coming from a very polite family, this was all rather more than I could cope with, but seemed quite normal to these village people. You got the impression that many of the marriages were more or less arranged, or maybe there just wasn't much of a choice. Either they ran out of suitable applicants, or they just gave up on trying to save me, as it all came to an eventual stop. I think they just thought all artists were crazy, well the three others I knew in the village were definitely a bit bonkers.

The first couple of summers, I spent most evenings down on the beach. Setting up a makeshift stall on the parade alongside others who made jewellery, various crafts, and several Africans selling ripped copies of music CD's. I would try to sell my paintings of local scenes to people staying on holiday in the hotels, who after having a good meal would go for a stroll. That was a plum time to try and convince them to take a painting home with them as a memory of their holiday. I get the feeling that more than a few realised too late that it would not fit in the suitcase. Over the course of the summer I did well, and made enough to keep body and soul together. It was also a really pleasant way to spend time, chatting, relaxing with the sun setting over the Mediterranean behind me. It also helped that I was friends with the Ice cream parlour just across the road. For light, later on, we just hooked into the local electricity supply or, in my case, used two old car headlamps, and a battery. My one problem was that the tourists were a bit disappointed that I was English and not Spanish. They wanted something authentic. So sometimes I would get a Spanish friend to do the sales patter, they were better than me at it, and more successful. On other occasions an African friend of mine who was good looking and with a flashing smile, would chat up all the young ladies, in an effort to make sales for me, but I think he had ulterior motives! Unfortunately, the local shops started complaining about loss of trade and the increase in African lucky, lucky men, so the council stopped it. Bit of a stupid decision as at the same time they were trying to encourage tourism. Apart from all the bars we were the only other entertainment on offer, except for a certain road at the back of the council offices.

The local bus driver lived in a nearby village, and was allowed to take his bus home with him every night. Once I saw him returning from a different direction at gone midnight with an awful lot of his extended family waving from the windows, and obviously in good spirits. It was a definite case of moonlighting; I bet his bosses didn't know. Anyway, his main official route lay over the mountains and eventually after a tortuous journey would arrive in the central bus station in Granada. This journey started at 6am and took several hours, because it visited all sorts of side villages. A relaxing calm journey viewing the landscape would have been quite nice, only he drove too fast around the mountain roads. He went around blind narrow bends without an apparent care in the world, and generally frightened the wits out of me. I only took the trip twice, after that I felt I was pushing my luck. About six months after I left, I heard that he had indeed gone off the road, luckily only into an orchard, flattening a couple of chickens on the way.

During rehabilitation for a knee operation I had to take a daily ambulance down to the nearest town. Jammed together with several old ladies in various states of health, the driver would bounce and rattle his way around all the mountain villages collecting even more patients. By the time we reached the

Physiotherapy Department we had been on the road for over two hours. The strain of keeping ourselves upright on the trip had given us enough muscle exercise for the day, and we still had the return journey to look forward to.

This is a bit rude, but too good to miss out. The next village Guaja Fondon put on a recital by the local ladies choir. Lots of lively Spanish numbers, by a fifty strong cast of mostly mature and fearsome looking women, in bright red flamenco dresses and vivid lip gloss. They were accompanied by a guitarist, but several of the ladies played a drum like container with a pole sticking out the top, which they pumped furiously up and down to make different farting like sounds depending on its size. I'm sorry but I was crying with laughter, not only at the sound, but the amazing wrist action. I looked around to see if I was the only one with a dirty mind, but was relieved to see that quite a number were valiantly trying to hide their sniggering. I think the ladies themselves knew quite well the reaction they were getting, and were enjoying the innuendo just as much. The evening was rounded off by great fun and dancing going on outside the church, into the early hours, and it was mostly the older folks who had the stamina to stick it out. The village was trapped in a time warp, during the day, quiet unchanged in years with just a few people shuffling about, but at night when the fiesta mood was on them, it came alive. It's a pity more tourists don't take the trouble to travel inland from the coastal resorts. These traditional villages are fascinating, and if you catch them during a fiesta you will never forget the memory, or the hangover.

I mentioned in the first book the two vicious storms that wiped out a couple of houses, washed away cars and completely demolished a swimming pool. Well even less powerful storms had an impact on the village, and particularly my part. After an hour or so of solid rain, the main street past my front door turned into a river. It often rose up the front step and on occasions high enough to pour into my hallway. Luckily we never used carpets, too much dust in these villages. On one occasion it rained so much that the fields on the slopes of the hill opposite were flooded, burst their embankments and poured brown water in a perfect arc right across the road. Cars could drive underneath and not get very wet. The torrent would proceed down a gully just to the side of my house and away down to the river bed. I was lucky, if the flood had accessed the road twenty feet to its left, it would have poured straight into my house.

Now I live in a cave house in a different part of Andalucía, it is so different, quiet and peaceful, but I kind of miss the vibrancy of that village. The old place had no garden, I was overlooked by neighbours, the street was noisy, my home was cold in winter and hot in summer, the winds often blew like gales around the corner, and the windows would rattle. But somehow I have fond memories and kind of miss it, despite having a lot of problems there. Now my cave house is spacious, quiet, not overlooked, with a reasonable ambient temperature all year. If I had to choose between the two places, the cave house would win hands down. There is nothing to complain about, and it's perfect for me, but yet it somehow lacks something. I think it's excitement. Nothing happens here; I have to drive to events, meetings, entertainment. My life seems split, everything happens away from my home. Actually this is something I would have wished for, and I do appreciate the calm of getting home after being out half the night. It's just a contradiction, and in true British spirit I am never satisfied with how lucky I am, or to be where I am.

That about wraps up any odds and ends, which got omitted from the first book. Especially about my first three years, when I resided nearer the coast. Since 2007, I have lived in my present home near Baza, some two or three hours inland. Comments and tales are more closely linked to this area from now on.

IN THE DARK

In England I don't ever remember being in the complete dark, but then again I lived in an ordinary house, in an ordinary street, in an ordinary town. So when the electricity went off the first time in my Spanish 'dug out of the hill' home, it was a new experience. It was night, and with little or no moon, plus half my rooms don't have windows. I was alone in my cave house in the middle of the campo, with no lights from other houses. It was literally pitch black; you could not make out your hand in front of your face. I wasn't scared there was nothing to fear, after all I was in my home and everything around me was still there, except I could not see it. I was more scared of the single mosquito I could hear whining its way around. I had just had my hair cut short, what if it settled on my bald pate and stuck its proboscis into my brain. Funny how you feel vulnerable, when your hair suddenly goes.

Anyway, I'm sitting here in the dark, I know it's not my trip switch, which always makes a loud click, it was silent and instantaneous. One moment you are blithely doing something, and the next second you are blindly groping for the nearest wall, which is never in the direction you sensed it was. You bang your knee on the chair, which was surely much more over to the left. So as I sat and waited for the guy on night duty at the local power plant to have his bit of fun and throw the main switch back on (it always helps to visualise someone to blame) I realised that we are never normally in complete darkness. We light up our roads and houses, or use a torch. Maybe when we are asleep it's black, but that does not count, I bet the insect repellent plug glows at the very least. To be suddenly in genuine darkness, particularly with 20 feet of earth above you, is quite a sobering experience. Especially without any means of improving the situation without crashing into every bit of furniture, on the hunt for that candle you know you put somewhere. It is probably at the other end of the cave system to the box of matches, they may not even light, because you have them on the shelf above the gas cooker. They will no doubt have absorbed way too much steam.

It kind of throws you back in time. What must it have been like when power, heat, and light were not readily available at the flick of a switch? Sitting in the dark I vowed to be more appreciative of these luxuries in the future. But most likely will just forget and continue to take them all for granted. But one thing I know for sure is that I would not swop my rustic hole in the hill, out in the middle of nowhere, for a smart furnished town house in any city.

The light came back on, funny how a forty watt bulb can suddenly look so bright. I found four dogs and a cat huddled on the sofa. Normally I leave a small light on for them, so suddenly being left in the dark, affected them as well. The only other time they huddle for support is when I start to sing and play my guitar.

The other consideration that came into my head, whilst I sat in the dark contemplating my situation, was that it was a metaphor for my original intention to come and live in Spain. My last few years in England, had at that time and still does, appear all black. Without going into details, it involved death, breakup and subsequent depression. Although I had now been in Spain for some time, waiting for the light to come on that night was like a symbol for a new start, everything that went before in my previous life in England was well and truly over and done with. From now on everything would be new. Blimey! That was a bit deep, sorry about that.

Oh well! Off to hunt down that candle.

Tabarca Island

GUIRES

Most Spaniards, except where we over proliferate, are willing to tolerate us foreigners. We are colloquially termed *guiris*, this derivation comes from the word *guirigay* which literally means gibberish! Funny how every nationality thinks they are the intelligent sensible ones. The Spanish don't really consider the block house jungle areas such as the Costa del Sol or Costa Blanca, to be really part of Spain. Some are new and without a past, others once had a proud history, but have been savagely changed by developers. In winter many are empty and closed up, barren and soulless, just silently brooding and waiting for the next mad rush of tourists. They are a fake paradise created solely for foreigners so that the Spanish can rook us of our holiday money, whilst we turn our pale skin bright red, get drunk on cheap booze, sit jammed together on a beach, swim in a sea polluted by the effluence of a hundred tall hotels, buy time shares and sing badly at karaoke evenings. In such places it's all part of the fun of the big picture for the Spanish. I was talking to a waiter I knew, who had retired from a bar catering for the British on the coast, he had come back to live with his family. He had bought a house purely on the proceeds of twenty years of tips. The man had made an art form out of smiling and joking with the tourists, as if they were actually his friends. 'It's all a game" he said, "and we are very good at it." Holiday resorts are not stupid and will gear themselves to a specific age range; hence retirement, holiday and adolescent fun are all individually catered for. You can't blame them, the area that I live in Andalucía, has been poor so long, it has given the region a new lease of life and the chance for at least a percentage of its population to find work on the coast.

Maybe it's the austerity of their past, but making money is very much to the forefront and done with quite a degree of pride. It comes into play all the time. If you make enquiries about buying a property, suddenly the price rises. The outbuildings and field at the back are not included and will cost you more. As I mentioned I had purchased my first home, only to find that the cellar was not included because it was the workroom of the man's son, who was a blacksmith. They think we are stupid, and therefore worthy of being conned. They do have a point, as many Brits come over with a dream and blindfolds, me included. One person I know was in negotiations to buy an abandoned manor house for half a million Euros. The place was semi derelict and would need that much again to restore it to its former glory. He said he would open it as a hotel, despite the fact that it was in the middle of nowhere, didn't have electricity, sewage system or even direct access. Notwithstanding the fact, that you can count the number of people who may need a hotel, on the fingers of your two hands in this area.

I have lost count of the number of people, particularly on Facebook who, just like me at the time, are overwhelmed with enthusiasm that they are moving out to sunny Spain. You can't blame them; it is a wonderful place to live, if you have some money. They make statements like; I am a plumber, carpenter, motor mechanic, builder, or any of another assortment of practical skills. The assumption is that what works in Britain will sustain them here. I can't speak for the areas such as Cataluña which are more organized, but in Andalucía, you would be extremely lucky, or charge very little, to get this sort of work, other than on your own restoration projects. The local Spanish have more or less sown up these types of jobs, after the entire unemployment rate around here is way over 25%. So lots of them become builders. Likewise one couple were going to open a craft shop, are you crazy, the Spanish are too busy having Fiestas or working hard, or with their large extended families, to worry about hobbies. Crafts are for lonely souls like myself. I know a couple of British that run bars, but you have to be very organised and willing to stay up half the night. There are never enough bars for the locals; however there is so much competition. Even our local village has fourteen of them. You can have a stall on the local car boot. Some Brits seem to make enough to survive, selling packed food from Britain, such as baked beans, marmite and Branston pickle. Or, if you can find quality cheap clothes, or enough regular house clearance junk to sell. If you speak good Spanish, then there is some possibility of translation work for the ex-pats. Apart from that there is really not much chance of regular work around here. Even if you have good qualifications, it will not get you work in a business office, school or the local council. Working for yourself is everyone's dream, but don't forget you have to register for tax purposes and it will cost you over 250 euros per month in social security payments, before you start to make any profit.

If you have plans to move out to Spain and still need to create an income, come out on exploratory trips. Find out exactly what is and isn't possible. Look at different areas, ask questions and speak to other people who have already done it. Stay for at least a couple of months, and see if you still like living here, but more to the point, is it possible. This makes perfect sense, but many don't seem to do it. (Including me, I talk from some experience, although I was very lucky).

I have seen many comments online especially by companies wanting your business and suggesting that Spain is very affordable and in fact one of the least expensive countries in Europe. Whilst there is a degree of truth in this, they are starting to stretch the real truth a bit. You may be able to buy a cheap property in the middle of nowhere, comparable to somewhere in the wilds in Britain, in which case the prices may be very similar. Try buying property in a Spanish city, nothing is cheap anymore. You can buy a ruin then spend the difference doing it up. The exchange rate of the euro and pound was very favourable, but at present there is not much between them, the gap is closing fast.

So what alternatives do you have?

Sell your overpriced house in Britain, come over, buy something cheap, if you can find something, and live off the profit margin for as long as you can.

Live off a pension and within your means. But remember at the time of writing this, Britain is in turmoil over Brexit. Spain is in turmoil over parts wanting to be independent, and claims of conspiracy at the highest level. So just how secure your pension is waits to be seen. All I know is that the recent events have taken their toll on the amount I have to live on.

Come over and adapt for any possible work, don't think you are secure in your chosen profession. I'm not saying it's not possible to follow your calling, just do your homework first.

Stay in England, looking out of the window at the rain, and forever regretting not taking the chance.

Spain is a paradise of socializing, culture and good health, just don't come here to make your fortune, or climb the career ladder.

The Expat Explorer Survey published by HSBC did a survey where they ranked 39 countries across the world on criteria such as quality of life, politics, career progression and health. Spain came 13th.

Having been a bit negative about your chances of finding work in my part of Spain, don't get put off if you have done your homework and know you can survive, you won't regret the experience. It is hard to see the gains when you are struggling to start again in a foreign country. Problems multiply and even the easy ones take on bigger proportions. However, never let them overshadow the fact that you are experiencing an adventure, one that most never have. If I could go back to the point before I made my decision to come here, and knowing what I've been through, I would 'Hell yes!' do it all again.

Acueduct Romano de Albanchez

ABOUT THE SPANISH

I have lived in this Country for thirteen years now. Along the way I have made some great Spanish friends, all who have been very kind to me. But it has dawned on me that no matter how hard I try, I will never be integrated. We share similar emotions, and sometimes beliefs, and even occasionally understand each other's jokes. But at the root of the problem is a different upbringing. We have learnt a different set of approaches to almost everything, not only from our parents, but historically as well. Even after all these years I find myself questioning what they are on about, why they think that way, and even what the hell are they doing, or not doing. We are not right and they are not wrong, it's just a difference of attitude. I am not talking so much about big issues such as injustice, poverty, social rights in general (although Spanish politics is an art form in its own right.) These big issues either appeal or repel in most nationalities in general. (With a few exceptions) It's the little things in daily life that highlight the differences. So here is a bit of opinionated information, be it right or wrong.

Firstly I need to defend myself, in most cases I am not making my own supposition here; much of the following has been explained to me by several Spanish friends from different regions. They did not start out being my opinions, but I have certainly seen a lot of the characteristics, since they have been pointed out to me.

There is definitely a touch of the over dramatic about the Spanish, although they definitely come second best to Italy. This is strange because they can also be highly laid back. It must be that much used phrase 'Latin blood'. Whereas, us from cooler climes, reside somewhere in the middle. Either we are mildly animated, or slightly sluggish. This is never more evident than watching Spanish television. The soaps have long pauses between each section of a confrontation, where the camera pans into a facial expression, which is held by the actor for two seconds longer than is natural. Even the weather reporter is agitatedly animated, rushing from side to side of the board, arms waving as they describe that it's going to be another hot day, just like the previous fifty. But way over in the corner of the map is a little rain cloud that just has to be pointed out five times. Newsreaders manage to keep their body under control almost as if it's in a vice, but their faces give free reign to stock expressions of anger, disbelief, concern and shared sadness about an event. Most of these have the aspect of having been learnt in the classroom for newsreaders. The latest newsreader on Andalucía Television, keeps flicking her hair out of one eye by quick shakes of her head, it's really annoying. But the prize has to go to any discussion programme, where a bunch of people have been dragged in to discuss the latest news event. They are meant to be experts, who therefore must understand the complexities of the situation. But they still seem able to totally disagree with each other. Normally they start off by allowing each other to have a say, but it usually ends up with over shouting, interruptions and the funniest scenario, when none of them will stop talking until they have said their piece. The women's chat shows are just as bad. The five people all talk at the same time, how can they actually listen to what each are saying.

I forgot the inane celebrity gossip shows. Where a bunch of minor celebrities sit discussing animatedly, the goings on that appear large behind them on a giant screen. The boring part is that it's the same three minutes of footage repeated over and over and over again. The newscasts are the same, is that the only camera man on duty, or did they run out of digital storage? (Doesn't sound as good as saying did they only have one roll of film, Ah! the good old days)

The Spanish of Andalucía are a very complex species, very spontaneous in their actions, but at the same time need everything to be routine and as near to the same, year after year. Despite Religion losing its hold, they are still deeply traditional. Some 71% of its population still sees itself as Catholic, but that does not mean the vast majority of them turn up at church each week.

I have mentioned about their hesitancy to change things. The fiestas go on at the same time each year; they always include the same events. Religious festivals proliferate and these also follow the exact blueprint of the years preceding. No wonder they don't bother with posters, they all know what's going to happen and when. Spaniards tend to do the same thing every day at the same time. Coffee is always at the precise hour, bars will be empty then suddenly packed, and then empty again. This has little to do with offices or businesses having the same coffee break time, as the majority in the bars are retired, work for themselves, or don't work at all. Lunch comes around early afternoon and they don't even consider going out to a club before 1am.

It's not just about daily routines either. Each year in Spain seems designed to be as similar to the last as possible with Spaniards going to the same beach for their annual holidays, meeting up with the same people, eating the same food and talking about the same things. They are reserved, but often exuberant. Friendly, in general, but just as likely to be cantankerous. They can be very gracious, but above all else they are often loud. The decibel level in Spanish restaurants and bars can be deafening, but it's woven into the fabric of their give-and-take lifestyle. Two or three TV screens compete with loudly hissing coffee machines and a host of loud locals. Over half the inhabitants of Spanish cities endure noise levels well in excess of the World Health Organisation's 'healthy' limit of 65 decibels. Most noise in towns is caused by traffic, lustily supported by pneumatic drills, jack hammers, mopeds (usually without silencers), car horns, alarms, sirens, radios, televisions, fiestas, fireworks, discos, bars, restaurants, incessantly barking dogs, loud neighbours and screaming children.

In Spain, a normal conversation is two people shouting at each other from a few feet apart (not surprisingly, Spaniards are terrible listeners).

If you ask a Spanish male what the real religion of his country is, you'd get a fairly unanimous answer: football. It is more than just a game to them and followed with a passion that is almost religious in nature. Unlike the English football team, who are generally derided for lack of ambition or talent, the Spanish national team are looked on as almost godlike. When they lose, which is not often in the past few years, the supporters go into mourning.

I have been told by a Spanish friend that Latin men are expert hedonists, and mainly interested in five things: Football, food, alcohol, talking about sex and gambling (not necessarily in that order). The main preoccupation is on having a good time and a zest for life.

Like most people they will heavily criticise their own Country, but beware any other nationality sticking the knife in. More than back home, where we may poke fun lightly out of areas of the country, i.e. the Cornish or anyone from Birmingham, the Spanish are really quite vicious in their opinions of various sections of their own country.(Sorry Birmingham, that's twice I have criticised you in my books, and I've never ever been there. I am sure it is a wonderful place.)

An old well

HABITS THAT COME HARD

Kissing someone is something us British like to do in private or if we have to greet our favourite aunt, it is a quick peck on the cheek. There is no way on earth we would kiss a relative stranger, let alone give them a hug. The most they would get would be a firm handshake or just a friendly nod of the head. The first embarrassing encounters when you come to Spain, and not knowing how intimate you should be, slowly give way to

"What the hell, lets slap this complete stranger on the back and give this lady two, or is it even three smackers on the cheek."

I'm still not sure if your lips are actually meant to make contact with their skin, or it's more of a cheek to cheek thing, but with sound effects. If anyone knows I would be interested. It could be that the more you know them, then the mouth comes into play. But I do know that sticking your tongue in their ear is a definite no no. Being much more intimate than you ever imagined does become more comfortable with time, and it certainly is a more sociable way to meet and greet. Having said that, it is still a strange feeling hugging a bloke who is taller than me, and has broader shoulders. I may think I am mentally liberated from old taboos, but I have my limits.

Something you begin to notice as you learn your new adopted language is that the rural Spanish don't have a problem with swearing. It often peppers their conversation and not in an embarrassing way. Leaving aside the type of Brit that can't find more expressive ways than using four letter words, most of us were brought up to at least try not to swear, unless we hit our thumb with a hammer. I remember being shocked the first time I heard a Spanish lady shouting at her son, and using slang words for part of the female anatomy to express her feelings. Since then it is common place to hear what we consider rude words dropped into everyday conversation. Or is that just Andalucía? Here in the campo the locals don't hold back from telling it like it is, and are not ones to mince their words. But this seems to be when they are holding forth on a subject. Being told you look like a donkey's arse today, is all par for the course.

I was told that I should always tip, that it was custom here in Spain. However that is a myth created to con the tourist out of more money. But the local Spaniards barely tip, they're not really mean, they just don't do it. They can be very generous with friends and not adverse to spending money, particularly on special occasions, but tipping, why? You have already paid for the service. On your name day, it is the custom to treat all your friends to at the least a drink. I don't think there is a Cedric or Clarence day, but there sure is a John Day, so being a tight bastard, I try to stay in then. Not only Saints days but also on your birthday, kind of gets a bit expensive if you are popular, thankfully I'm not.

The family is a strong bond in Spain, swooning over random babies in shops and in passing on the street, seems to be a traditional pastime. Children are treated like royalty, and the word "Guapa" is used liberally, even if the kid is obviously not. Fussing over babies, pinching their cheeks and smothering them with kisses can be really annoying when you're waiting in line to be served. Even strangers seem to take an interest in other people's kids, not something I suggest you practice when you go back to England. It is on record that Spain is one of the best places in the world to be a mum. Apparently they look after their children so well that they don't want to leave, particularly in the case of boys who prefer to stay until at least the age of 30, or until they marry a woman who can take over from their mother.

The Spanish seem to prefer eating late. They may consume lunch between two and four but don't even think about dinner until 9pm at the earliest. This takes a bit of getting used to, especially as most British, don't like going to bed on a full stomach. In Spain, life is savoured, with time taken to enjoy life's pleasures. People stroll the streets in the evenings, enjoying the long evenings and chatting with neighbours and partake most meals together quite late. However, we think we need to be in bed by midnight, in case we actually may enjoy ourselves, God forbid!

Do not be alarmed by a dirty floor in a bar. It is completely acceptable and normal to throw things on the ground in bars. Most of the time a dirty floor means a good bar! Spain has the second highest number of bars per inhabitants, the only country that has more bars than Spain is Cyprus. Bread is present and required at almost every meal, even if you have a big plate of chips and potatoes.

Spaniards appear to be sticklers for following strict seasonal rules. Despite the fact that it's still swelteringly hot in much of the country in September and even well into October, all the outdoor swimming pools close their doors at the end of summer. Winter rules also apply: even if the beginning of December is quite balmy, Spaniards will make sure they are wrapped up and Spanish grannies wear their fur coats until the official end of winter in late March.

Promising to call back or saying it will be here by Wednesday and doing neither seems to be a common practice. This may be the same in England now, but it's been so long since I lived there. I don't know if they are just trying to please, but it is very annoying. If they can't get it or don't intend phoning, then why not just say so. They are going to lose my custom either way in the end so at least be honest. There is a certain delivery company whose name rhymes with the word Sewer, who are notorious for non-delivery of parcels in this area, they make no effort to find you especially if you live in the campo. The first thing you know is that your packet has been returned to Britain, or even America. I think we should club together and buy them a sat-nav system. Mind you where I live it's like a Spanish version of the Bermuda triangle. Google earth it and scan down, it gets more and more blurred until it ends up as a rather arty geometric design in autumn colours.

The assumption that because you know thirty Spanish words and can mix them with sign language, facial contortions and English words that somehow sound Spanish if you add a letter or two and elongate it at the end, (as in "wante" or "problemaah"),then the locals see no need to slow down with their responses. It is often the case that requests to slow down, produce the opposite effect and they actually speed up. We compound the problem by nodding or using "Si", ten times a minute, when actually we understood very little. It can be very dangerous; you never know what you are getting yourself into. The word yes at the wrong moment could cause you all sorts of trouble and strife.

The Spanish are increasingly getting into Christmas, although it was always a low key affair, coming a long way down in importance as a fiesta to the Three Kings day, which takes place in the first week of January. It seemed strange in the first few years I was over here when you could not find a Christmas card to buy, there were no street decorations, no houses had fairy lights in their windows and Christmas Day was just like any other to all intense and purposes. That is changing and there will soon come a time when I think that they will realise that they have a good excuse to join up both celebrations in one long fiesta stretching over a good couple of weeks. Having spent my life expecting to get bloated on a large Christmas dinner, I was seriously disappointed when an invitation from Spanish friends ended up with cheese, ham, and chips with a fried egg. A couple of years ago we had a Christmas meal booked by a few dozen of us at a local bar. It was strange seeing two dozen Brits eating ham, cheese and olives, not just me. Bravely the next year a friend Ken took over the kitchen of another bar and produced a traditional Christmas meal.

Nowadays, you can buy all the normal Christmas crap including climbing Santa's, and the TV is full of endless children's games they want to sell you. Most are plastic and will be broken by Boxing Day. There was an advert for one game called Og on the bog. It comprised of a troll sitting on the bog in a wooden outside toilet. You had to pinch his toilet paper before his arse exploded. God give me strength! What next, catch the vomit? I once had a craft stall next to a guy who was busy selling mirrors with a dartboard painted on them, they were called zit mirrors, and I don't think I need to go into details of the rules of the game. In a few hundred years they will dig up the layers of plastic garbage in landfill sites and wonder about our culture. Some future Baldric will stand smiling at the camera in a programme called Ye Oldie Merry Europe Time Team, whilst holding up a plastic figure of a Belen crapper

(see page 44) that he has just dug up and suggesting that around the year 2000 toilets hadn't been invented. That is until the fat hairy one produces Og on the bog to refute the argument. (sorry got carried away there)

DAMA DE BAZA

STORIES FROM OTHERS

Your first responses to my request for interesting stories in Spain, part 1.

From Susan We bought our villa off plan. Once moved in and having experienced our first winter in Spain, which included much snow, I complained to the builder that our central heating radiators weren't big enough. He looked at me quite bemused and said "there's nothing wrong with the size of your radiators; it's just that your rooms are too big!"

From Alison We've only been here 5 months & we needed to do some DIY. So my husband and I went to the hire shop to get a compressor. The guy serving spoke really good English and asked my husband if he was sure what he was ordering. The guy then asked what he wanted it for and my husband explained that he wanted to repaint a large area. The guy again looked at my husband and said 'Would a brush not be easier than a tampon?' (Being English we say compress-a as opposed to compress-or)!!!

From Maggie In our local bar I asked for the key to the toilet using my best Spanish and using sign language. Eventually she nodded and went in the kitchen and brought out a bowl of alioli.

From Mary I was giving a private English lesson to a young girl who was very afraid to make mistakes because she thought it made her look silly. I told her not to worry about it because learning a language required being a bit of a fool. She never came back for another lesson. I later learned that I had mistakenly translated the English word "fool" into the Spanish word "fulana". I had in fact told her that to learn a new language she had to be a bit of a whore.

From Sarah A friend of mine took her 5 year old on holiday. He got an infection in his little Winky and need medical attention as he could not wee. So she asked around where there was a clinic and was directed to the nearest one. The lady in there didn't understand what she was being told, so my friend put her toddler on the counter pulled his underwear down so he could be looked at. Only to find out she was in an eye clinic.

From Kathy We found a young bird on our patio. Couldn't identify it so phoned a friend who is an ornithologist who still couldn't identify it from the description. He told us the mother would probably be looking for it and that it probably wouldn't eat anything. But there it was, happy to peck at some oats and water. A friend came down, and asked where the baby chicken had come from.

From Linda A cockerel turned up in my garden, but looked quite sick, so I took him to the Spanish vet, who told me he would die eventually, I told the vet would he please put him to sleep, the vet could not contain his laughter, nor could the 5 Spanish people in the surgery, but I still asked for him to do it. I stroked his head while he fell asleep, paid my 40 euro and left. I could still hear the laughing as I got in the car and must admit all my Spanish friends still find it funny. That was 17yrs ago, but I would still pay to have him put down now. (Yes, so would I)

A friend of mine named Patrice, made a comment about the Heineken baseball cap I was wearing. She comes from Holland like the lager, so commented "Hey you have a Dutch cap on your head." Not realising what she had just said, she was baffled why everyone was creased up laughing. After a careful explanation, she saw the funny side of it and amusingly tells others of her mistake. It certainly brings a strange image to mind every time I think about it. If it was big enough at least it would keep the rain off my bald spot.

FROM DAVE Once, on returning from a trip to Morocco, and badly in need of a wash, I caused great amusement by asking for 'sopa' in a Pharmacia. They looked puzzled especially when I indicated that I wished to wash under my arms. They explained that you do not wash with soup but rather soap, or in Spanish Jabon. On offering me some high priced fragrant soap I declined and proceeded to a convenience store where I once again caused great amusement by now asking for ham to wash under my arms. (Jamon). I am glad to say my Spanish and my personal hygiene have improved since then.

BILLIE I went to hospital for a CT scan, what we refer to as a cat scan in the UK. I'd worked out what I had to say in Spanish. However at the desk my Spanish completely left me I could say my name is in Spanish but couldn't for the life of me remember to say Cat scan, so I meowed at the receptionist and pointed from head to toe. The poor lady looked so confused, yet the man behind her literally fell about laughing at me. When I had a Doh! Moment and realized that it's actually a TAC scan in Spain and I had just meowed like a cat at this poor lady. I couldn't speak to my husband as I was laughing so much.

FROM **CHRIS** When in the butchers I couldn't remember the name for breast of chicken so I rubbed my hands over my breasts and said 'de pollo'. The guy thought it was so funny. Pechuga de pollo is now ingrained!

FROM **ALAN** We found the home of our dreams, put the deposit down and returned to England, very happy. The only trouble was that the next time we came over we could not find it, despite driving round and round the area. Obviously eventually we did, but our friends played a trick on us by sending a photo of themselves outside our purchase, with a new for sale sign behind them. It was a windup; they had taken a sign from down the road. Our home needed a lot of work, particularly the roof; it was badly leaking and seemed to be held together with mud. It bowed badly and numerous tiles were loose or gone. Deciding to repair it, I found it was the habitat of numerous small creatures. Jose an old guy from down the road would drag his chair along to watch my progress and make various comments, a hobby a lot of the old Spanish with time on their hands seem to have taken up. Throwing down a harmless blind slow worm to him, he promptly killed it with his walking stick, proclaiming it to be blood sucking vermin. My wife had stronger words for me when a rather large centipede dropped on the bed and proceeded to wander about under the covers, whilst she was occupying it.

I took my car for its annual test and was handed a walkie talkie, before the tester disappeared into the pit beneath my vehicle. Unfortunately knowing very little Spanish and also hindered by the fact that his voice sounded like it was coming from the bottom of the ocean , every command to turn the steering wheel, press the brakes or any other such instructions were promptly acted upon by me doing the completely wrong thing. I think he just gave up in the end and passed me.

After congratulating Fina our Spanish friend who is over 50 years old, on being pregnant, I discovered that it was her daughter they were talking about.

We gave a biscuit to a poor donkey that was tied to a large rock. Having done our good deed we turned away and headed for our house. However, the donkey had decided that it rather liked biscuits, and no rock was going to stop it trying to get another, so it simply dragged the rock behind it and headed after us. The problem was that the direct route lay across ours and Manuel our neighbour's garden. Ploughed fields can look quite attractive, but not when it's a furrow across flower beds.

I was telling a very nice girl that she had a Bonita Pero, instead of Bonita Perro. Later I thought that what I had said was she had a very nice butt. Luckily the American slang term of Butt did not equate. If I had said she had a nice culo then I would have been due a slap.

INTERESTING FACTS

Spain is only one of four nations with a National Anthem that has no lyrics (the others are San Marino, Kosovo, Bosnia & Herzegovina). The anthem is thought to be one of the oldest in the world; it was first seen in a manuscript back in 1761

Due to the tradition of naming your child after its own grandfather, if you call somebody Paco, you have a one in four chance of being right.

Only a short time ago Iceland changed its law, which let you kill Basque people legally.

It is apparently an accepted tradition to show if a meal has been enjoyable, by dropping your napkin on the floor, after wiping you mouth and hands. This was considered quite normal practice in the past and in most bars I have been in still seems to continue, judging by the mess. It's strange because people spend hours scrubbing out their own apartments with bleach (My friend does), and would never dream of going out in public looking less than immaculate.

Often the names of famous authors, musicians and actors are interestingly changed from our perspective. An example of this would be the copy of Oliver Twist by Carlos Dickens.

Felipe Colines (Phil Collins)
Prince Charles is Prince Carlos
Queen Elizabeth is Queen Isabel
Prince Andrew is Andres

The Pope is Juan Pablo in Spain, mind you that's better than what they call him in Maori   (Ko Te Popa Hoani Pāora Te Tuarua)

In an introduction to one of Spanish speaking writer Jorge Luis Borges' books, he complains that the Spanish Academy had decided that "Viking" should be changed to "vikingo". He commented that if they had their way, "we will soon be reading the about Rudyard Kiplingo." Sounds more like an Ethiopian marathon runner.

Spanish people love the Christmas Lottery. From September until December there are queues daily in Madrid for the "El Gordo de Navidad". This is the Country's big national lottery and means "the fat one". It started in 1812 and is the second longest continuously running lottery in the world. Neither, a Civil War, or a dictatorial regime could stop it.

They are very accomplished swearers; some of the Spanish expressions for sex are also pretty colourful (fancy rubbing the spring onion anyone?).

As a rule, Spaniards really don't like being alone for more than a short time .The Spanish are known for their close family ties, it is to a degree the foundation of their society. They care and love their children and look after and respect their elderly, few are abandoned in nursing homes.

Don Quixote, the famous book written by Miguel Cervantes in 1605, was voted "The most meaningful book of all time" in 2002, by a panel of 100 top authors, including Salman Rushdie, and Normal Mailer.

Spain has the third most UNESCO World Sites out of all the countries in the World (after China and Italy) with 45.

Spain sits at the far-western edge of its time zone, so in high summer it's still light outside at 10 p.m.

Unemployment is still very high in Spain, the second highest in the EU. Recent economic problems and worsening of regional differences, means Spain is not the best place to come for job security.

Spain is renowned for its healthy Mediterranean diet full of fresh vegetables, fish and olive oil. But its consumption of wine tends to moderate the good effects. The food varies regionally; Basque and Catalan cooking may be the most renowned in Spain. But Galicia's seafood is superb, and eat paella in Valencia; aficionados say the reason is Valencia's water.

A survey of Spanish men revealed that they apparently make love on average about 71 times a year, which is down on the world average, which at the moment stands at 109. So that's once every five days or so, and presumably at weekends. They are also apparently quite bad at it. But what macho Spanish man is going to admit to that. I suppose the people who did the survey just spoke to their wives and girlfriends, to get the truth.

Spain lays claim to having invented many things, here are some that will probably be argued against, but there is at least some degree of truth in the claims.

Juan de la Cierva certainly went further than Leonardo de Vinci and constructed an early autogiro, and Isaac Perals was brave enough to descend in a Submarino long before most anyone else dared do it.

A lot of discoveries were the direct influence of the inquiring minds of the Muslim influence in Southern Spain during the five hundred or so years they were in occupation. Pure Alcohol distillation (Alchemist and physician Arnold of Villanova), and antiseptics (10th century Islamic hospitals had it.)

Ibn Hazm (994 to 1064) deserves to be far more famous. He is credited with inventing eye glasses, the metronome, water and weight driven clocks, and a process for creating artificial crystals.

A brass type movable printing press was invented in Spain a hundred years before Johannes Guttenberg took all the praise in 1454. Glass mirrors were used in Spain in the 11th century, 200 years prior to the Venetians. Tungsten was supposedly discovered in 1783. And the first calculator to subtract, multiply, divide and compute results up to fifteen digits was constructed by Ramon Silvestre Verea Garcia in 1878.

There are plenty more claims, and as I have said they are probably all open to question. One last amusing one is the claim that a physicist calculated the speed of sound by timing the echoes in the Mosque in Cordoba.

A DIVIDED COUNTRY

Bearing in mind that just back in the 1930s it was a deeply divided Country, torn between right-wing Nationalist and left-wing Republican, hence a civil war. Recent violent events have shown that Catalonia is desperate for independence and the Basque Country will not be far behind if Catalonia does separate. The Galician's are somewhat derided as being more like Portuguese than Spanish, and as for where I live, the Andalucian's are mocked by other parts of Spain, as just being peasants. This no doubt derives from the fact that not that long ago before mass tourism, they were ruled over by absent landlords who owned most of the land, but would not deem to live there themselves, paying very low wages to their workers. Originally, the Country consisted of eight Countries that got forced together over history. This process was called Reconquista.

The origin of the name España, referring to the whole Country as one autonomous area is uncertain; important parts are the Basque Country (País Vasco), the Catalan-Valencian-Balearic area, and Galicia, each of these has its own distinct language, and a strong separate identity. Other sections such as Andalucía; Aragón; Asturias; Castile; Extremadura; León; Murcia and Navarra, also have different identities, but in general speak understandable forms of Spanish. The land is divided into fifty provinces, and is grouped into seventeen autonomous regions, the basic political units of the Spanish population. Local areas, what we would know as neighbourhoods (*barrios*) are rooted in differences of perceived cultural heritage, deriving from their individual folklore and separate symbolism.

The ones who feel least like being Spanish are definitely the Catalans and Basques. The Basque language is totally unique, it bears no resemblance to any present day language, or for that matter any previously existing, but now extinct form. No wonder they see themselves as separate. Cataluña has more experience of autonomy, and in a way actually aligns itself just as much with

France as it does with the rest of Spain, having suffered periodic repression. They also have their own language, which is part Spanish with various Romanesque influences. Due to the rise of new passions for independence, their language is ousting official Spanish in many areas. Spain as we understand it has mostly been under the influence of Castile, an area that includes much of the Spanish Meseta. The marriage of Isabel to Fernando of Aragón in 1469 started the development and construction of modern Spain. Francisco Franco's regime (1939–1975) actually banned official use of the Catalan and Basque languages. The colours, yellow and red, used in the national flag were first adopted in 1785. But due to the countries changing and volatile past their national flag has only been displayed on public buildings since 1908.

Although they realise the economic necessity of united arrangements, there are too many differences, people have told me. This reflects in the recent news, Cataluña and the Basque Country being the most insistent on separation. Although, Spaniards are often disparaging about their compatriots from other regions. The most widespread antagonism is between the cities of Madrid and Barcelona, whose inhabitants argue about everything, including the economy, sport, history, politics, culture and language. Catalans claim that *Madrileños* are half African, to which they reply that it's better than being half French. Each is proud of their regional identity.

Although not as defined as the British or French class systems, Spain has a class structure. At the top are the aristocrats or Grandees, below them come numerous minor nobles. Then comes, the middle class professionals, the white-collar workers, the blue-collar workers and lastly the peasant underclass and finally the Gypsies (Gitanos), who seem to be hated even more than drunken tourists. Amongst the Gypsies, only famous flamenco artists or bullfighters are celebrated by the rest of Spain.

MORE STRANGE FIESTAS

After mentioning the crazy baby jumping festival of Castillo de Murcia, near Burgos, in the last book, where grown men dressed as devils jump over new born babies. I decided to hunt down some others as it seemed if somebody can come up with an idea, then the Spanish are definitely up for it, especially if it means partying hard. In a small village near Granada, the population pile tons of burning twigs in the alleyways and narrow streets to celebrate San Antoñio their Patron Saint. Giant flames rise up under wooden balconies whilst the designated fire fighters stand around calmly.

At Las Hogueras de San Juan they burn small versions of Las Fallas. When the fire fighters put out the fires at the end, it's traditional to insult them in such a disrespectful way, that they traditionally start spraying water into the crowd.

This one is more of a tradition than a fiesta. Caga Tió (the shitting log) is a supposedly friendly twig of wood, which is meant to grow during December as you feed it. Finally as a log with a smiley face, it poops out Christmas gifts when you beat it with a stick, whilst children entice it to 'shit some presents' by singing. (Don't ask me to explain, I just find the information) The Caganer figurine which is to be generally found in traditional Christmas nativity scenes is meanwhile taking a dump in the corner.

Los Indianos, or the Indians, is a Carnival festival in which thousands of Palmeros dress up in white and parade on the streets. The main aim seems to be to chuck talcum powder all over each other. It goes on for ages and must be a nightmare from anyone suffering from a sensitive nose. How this originated seems to have come from tales of the early settlers in Latin America that sailed over from the Canary Islands. Talcum tossing is symbolic of the powders sprinkled over the travellers to avoid any chance of spreading viruses.

Near Alicante is something similar but in this case it is flour, the Els Enfarinats festival, spares nobody, including the police, so if you want to get your own back, you know where to go.

I have mentioned the dead rat throwing festival at El Puig before, but I did not realise that they start their festivities by distributing Pinates, (I'm not sure what they are, but think you are meant to eat them) some are filled with sweets and candy, but others are filled with frozen rodents, Yuk!

Batalla Del Vino (battle of the wine) in Haro, hosts local fights, with much spilling and hurling of wine in all directions. But this is the La Rioja region, so they have plenty of it, although it seems a shame to waste so much of a good wine.

. In the Basque fishing village of Lekeito they suspend a dead goose on a rope over the harbour. Young men then attempt to leap from small boats and grab the bird which has been well greased. The inevitable happens and most miss and end up in the water. If they manage to grab the bird and hang on, spectators on the quayside who are controlling the rope shake it violently to loosen their hold, or just dunk them in.

Something less energetic but not without a little pain, involves the young unmarried women of Madrid visiting the Chapel de San Isidro and pricking their fingers with a pin then placing it in a blessed vessel, in order to find a husband. Not quite as efficient as internet dating, but I guess anything's worth trying if you are that desperate.

HEALTH

Between odd amusing information, serious topics and your tales, I will continue to add self-opinionated chapters about anything that amuses, irritates or generally happens to me. This is one about health issues. I thank God for the Spanish health system it has given me so much to write about.

THE DENTIST

When the dentist told her she had to have a tooth out, she replied I'd rather have a baby.

The dentist replied, "Make up your mind; I've got to adjust the chair."

I once had a dentist in Britain whose hobby was archaeology. Not content with spending his week digging into people's mouths, he spent weekends and holidays digging into the earth. Everyone is allowed to follow their interests as long as it does not harm anyone. But I thought it was a bit much that all around the surgery, in plain view to any patients trapped in the dental chair were photographs of him rooting away with a trowel and even worse hitting large rocks with a massive pickaxe. It did not exactly inspire much confidence. I asked him once if he had put them up intentionally, to my surprise he said that he had not seen the connection. Either he was having a secret joke, or he was seriously lacking in imagination, either way the omens did not seem good for my root extraction.

The reason this subject is finding its way into the book, is that not for the first time this year I have toothache. Why does it always happen on a Sunday, so unless you want to spend a small fortune, or trust your luck at the hospital accident and emergency, you just have to ride it out overnight with the help of half a bottle of whisky and a packet of out of date paracetamol. Worse still it is Cascamora week in Baza, our local town, ten days of fiesta, where just about everything closes up, including most of the dentists. The last known sighting of my dentist was of her running down the hill, covered from head to foot in black liquid, and slapping handprints on any object or person that got in her way. They sure have some funny fiestas in Spain. People give me good advice, like jump in the car and head for another town that isn't celebrating something, but I just like to suffer, so I can moan later, or like now as I'm writing this.

A few months back I had to have the roots from a big old molar killed and removed. God or whoever created me was not content with just giving me giant feet, a curved spine and short sight, apparently my roots were the longest and toughest she had ever seen. My dentist broke three of her tungsten files clearing them out, and spent nearly five hours with her knee in my chest. The night before I had consumed rather a lot of beer, and it was not surprising that half way through the procedure, I suddenly needed to go. This would have been ok but she had somehow attached some kind of small green tent over my mouth. Spring wires protruded in different directions, and the plastic membrane was stretched right over my mouth and held down all around the single protruding bad tooth that poked through. Mouth pinned wide open, all I could do was mutter unintelligible phrases and point to my trouser zip area. Complete with green flowing gown, and a massive contraption obscuring the lower half of my face, and no doubt dribbling because it was impossible to swallow, I made my way past the row of people waiting their turn. I think one or two of them may then have had second thoughts about their loose filling. Two minutes later I passed by on the way back, there were definitely less people sitting waiting. Settling back I relaxed and prepare to cope with two more hours in that chair. Did I also mention that I have a small bladder, yes I had to repeat the trip once more, I didn't look at the people waiting, due to acute embarrassment.

A man visits his dentist because his mouth feels weird. His dentist examines him and says, "That new upper plate is eroding. What have you been eating?"

"All I can think of is that I love Hollandaise sauce, I put it on everything: meat, toast, fish, vegetables, everything."

"Well," the dentist says, Hollandaise sauce is made with lots of lemon juice, which is highly corrosive. It's eaten away your upper plate. I'll make you a new plate, and this time use chrome."

The patient asks, "Why chrome?"

The dentist replies, "It's simple. Everyone knows that there's no plate like chrome for the Hollandaise."

Whether you're visiting or living in Spain, Dentists in Spain are mostly private and not covered by the Spanish healthcare system. Thus there is no free dental care in Spain except for children and emergency treatment for adults, such as extractions. This means that if you need routine treatment for your teeth in Spain you will have to pay, or take out private dental health insurance. Dentists in Spain tend to be more affordable than in some neighbouring countries. When visiting the dentist in Spain, all you need to do is make an appointment beforehand, and you must show some form of ID on arrival. Although initial consultations, teeth examinations and some aftercare check-ups are typically free, you will have to pay for the rest, unless you're aged between 6 and 15 years old .Always ask for a quote if you are going to have a course of treatment. For example, some procedures are half the price of dental treatment in the UK, which is why Spain has become a popular dental tourism destination. However this may all change soon with Brexit, but who knows. If you have an emergency dental problem, go to the Emergency Departments in your nearest hospital.

My dentist says dental work is not brain surgery, unless he slips.

I had a plate made with several false teeth projecting from its metal edge. I was decidedly cheaper than having more permanent solutions, and all I could afford at the time. Being somebody who hates wearing rings, watches or even glasses because they make me somewhat claustrophobic, having a plate in my mouth was and still is a nightmare, it feels alien. Friends say just leave it in, you will get used to it, but I just can't, so the moment I get home from anywhere, out it comes. Now I am also quite careless, so my offending dentures often get lost. Normally they are in the house, such as down the sofa or on top of the fridge, in a random cup, or even my coat pocket. But a couple of occasions it has been rather more embarrassing. I took them out to wash in the sink of my local bar, because there were bread crumbs under the plate. Sitting with my beer surrounded by the locals, I had to face the guy who came out of the toilet waving my false teeth in the air, and asking loudly if anyone had lost them. Another time I was driving through Granada, busy with traffic and I had a bit of toothache and the plate was chaffing, so I pulled them out and with no time to take my eyes of the road, I plonked them down on the passenger seat. I was going to pick up a female friend and yes you guessed it. As I pulled up she opened the car door and jumped in, and sat on my teeth.

I have a cavity: *Tengo una cari*

The needle will cause a slight sting: *La aguja le causará una picadura. (Don't believe them)*

Back in the 1950s, an 18-year-old girl from the northern town of León saw a classified advertisement for a secretary, applied for the position, and got it. Her boss then fell in love with her, but her father wouldn't let them get married, so she moved back to her hometown. Her love followed her and after marrying, they decided to start their own business. And that business turned out to be Spain's only false teeth factory.

A suspected thief was tracked down by police after he left his false teeth at the crime scene. When he tried to make a quick getaway, he was found by using dental records and the police charged him. A Police spokesman reported, 'He tried to tell us that while the false teeth were his, they had been stolen from him. He had not been anywhere near, but we knew he was lying through his dentures.'

My dentist informs me that despite having no pain, I have an abscess in my upper gum and will probably have to lose three of my remaining teeth that I can genuinely say are mine, and then a whole new upper plate fitted. She told me this whilst smiling broadly, and suggesting it may come to 1,500 euro including something called plasma filling. Where they grow an alien life form extracted from something and mix with your blood, Yuk! Anyway at this precise moment I am writing this paragraph in the car park of Brico Depot in Granada. I have just purchased a load of wood that I don't actually need at the moment, certainly not to shore up my gums. The reason is that I have just driven to Granada for a scan on my upper jaw. Luckily I phoned whilst sitting here to confirm the appointment, which they announced they had no record of. "Come tomorrow,' they said. "Not likely," I said whilst explaining that it was some distance from Baza, and as it was their fault, they needed to fit me in today. After a lot of back room discussion they told me to come later, so now I have three hours to waste and hence why I went and purchased the wood for something to do. Rather than drink endless coffees in a bar, I am also now writing this on the back of a couple of old receipts found under the driver's seat and using an old stubby pencil that I have had to pick at to reveal enough lead to write with. I have also done two little pen drawings with a leaking biro that has just been chucked in the bin, after covering two fingers with black ink. Next I will be forced to go and look around Conforama, and no doubt be tempted into buying something for the home, even if it's just a tea towel.

Thinking about the cost of a new set of dentures, has anyone got an old packet of slightly off white FEMO. You know the stuff that hardens naturally after you have made a passable attempt at modelling a Smurf. It would be a lot cheaper to construct my own set, as long as I don't smile much, I should be able to get away with it.

Well that was fun! I had the scan, apart from waiting in line to register with the receptionist where you had to pay in advance in case you tried to sneak out with your x rays without paying. It meant that I was three quarters of an hour late entering the scan room. They didn't seem to care, so much for having an appointment. When the scan was finished I waited for the files. The operator came out with a baffled expression and stared at my face. He said something about me not having any bruises. Then he asked me if somebody had punched me in the face recently.

I don't think I have an abscess, more likely a trauma, but you can bet your life it is still going to cost me the same for treatment, you just know it. Now I am trying to remember the last time that somebody punched me.

YOUR STORIES, PART TWO

From POP I went to the Correos to see if there was any post for us, there were two women in there who said I had a bright shirt. Is it him? Pedro the postman asked '¿Tocas guitarra? (do you play guitar)', I said 'Si', and he handed me an envelope addressed to 'El hombre Inglés que lleva camisas de colores brillantes y toca la guitarra, Cortes de Baza, Spain' (The guy with the colourful shirt who plays guitar). It caused much amusement and Pedro insisted we had our photo taken with the envelope. It was from our Nathan who wanted to see how much we'd integrated. Since then the story has appeared in the local press and on TV, I'm now officially a celebrity.

We were in a village 16km away having coffee when my chair collapsed. One old boy, who looked like he had dropped in and out in 1968 and never left, with long white hair and a white droopy moustache, nipped over to help me up. Later we got chatting 'you play guitarra' - I said 'yes' but how he knew this I don't know. It turned out he lived in a cave 8 klms along the river, but he knew I played guitar. I asked if he played guitar too, 'No, I play piano but I have no piano, they are very expensive in Spain'. I said I knew a few musicians, and would ask around. Then he told me he used to live in a village, Macael, past Tijola, about 60 klms away, which was famous throughout Spain for its marble, and there was a hall there, completely made of marble, the walls and the floor were all marble, and there was a piano there and when he played it the whole place seemed to be alive and the walls sang with the sound of the piano, the marble made it sound so good. All of this was with big gesticulations, wide eyes and deep feeling. He also told us about the rogue piece of 500 ton marble which rolled down a hill, but which he managed to outrun. A lovely, lovely man, his name is Rodrigo, and we hugged each other when we left and said we were amigos. Things like that which have happened a few times to us, is part of the reason we love Spain. So now we're looking for a piano for Rodrigo.

From Simon

My neighbour Simon achieved a degree of notoriety by appearing in a photographic exhibition, in which he dressed up as a Red Indian complete with tomahawk, and proceeded to dance around our local quarry at night whilst the cameraman produced laser light effects around him. I bet that was the first time our little pueblo experienced anything like that. It is usually just paella and an old guy doing Frank Sinatra impersonations at the annual fiesta. However, here are a couple of other incidents he has allowed me to publish.

Whilst renting a place in another part of Spain, he got into serious altercations with the landlord. At one point he was threatened with violence, when the man turned up with others. To get the full benefit of this incident you have to have an image of Simon. He has several ear adornments and tattoos on his body, and even on his skull and face. He is also very interested in native cultures, as well as making a lot of traditional leather clothing such as boots and moccasins. So I suppose you could truthfully say that he has his own style and does not look like the average bloke in the street. Apart from making impressive walking sticks, carved like totem poles he also made a bow and arrows. Now we come to the part where the police turned up to interview him about the incident.

"Now sir, they say that you were firing at them with a bow and arrows?"

"Yes"

"They said you had lots of tattoos, they could tell because you had no clothes on."

"yes"

So you were completely naked and firing arrows at them?"

"yes"

Apparently at this point the police had to go outside, because they could not contain their laughter anymore. After they calmed down, they came back in and completed the interview.

Another time he was taking a shower on a campsite when a group of youths came into the toilet block and started kicking all the cubicle doors, They had been pestering and somewhat frightening the locals prior to this. Simon kept on showering, when a lad kicked his door open. On seeing my friend in all his glory, and unconcerned about the intrusion, the lads jaw dropped and he uttered profuse apologies and retreated. When Simon came out of the shower block, they were sitting on a nearby wall all quiet and sheepish. It turns out they thought he was part of the local mafia.

From Linda

We were at the beach and had parked at the side of an approach to that beach. When we returned the car was stuck in the sand! Along came 4 beautiful Spanish girls. Maybe aged about 20. They called out to us 'are you stuck'? Yes we were! They pushed us out of the sand and called after us to have a lovely day! We so appreciated there help. If only they had seen that my hubby is 6ft 4in tall and 20st. They were pushing quite a weight!

From Sophie

I have a friend, who at the time enjoyed the odd glass or two of alcohol, although I believe she as now vowed to abstain. An invitation to sample the product of a friends moonshine (yes you can buy stills locally, if you thought that moonshine stills only existed in the hillbilly states of America,) was too tempting. As the powerful liquid dripped from the vibrating copper contraption it was readily sampled. The obvious result that they both got a bit plastered, and succumbed to a fairly inebriate state where most parts of the body refused to do what they were told. Staggering home in the early hours of the morning on a somewhat freezing winter's night, my friend realised that she did not have the keys to her front gate, which happened to be rather tall, and pointed at the top. Unperturbed she attempted to climb over. Unfortunately, reaching the top she got stuck and ended up hanging at a precarious angle from the gate, ripping her jeans from crutch to ankle. Being somewhat four sheets to the wind, she hung there for some considerable time, with the real chance of catching pneumonia or slowly succumbing to hyperthermia. Feeble cries for help remained unanswered, until some strangers wandering home late spotted her. With some assistance from them and a neighbour, my friend was restored to a vertical position.

My friend is not without inspiration. It is true to say that she likes chickens. Rather than leave them behind, she took two on a recent trip to the coast, where they played happily on the sand. Just to prove it here is a selfie.

LISTS

I like creating lists I do them most days and they cover things like what I am going to do today, this week, month, year and possibly the rest of my present existence. The fact that I hardly ever complete even the daily to do list doesn't stop me from enthusiastically producing a fresh one the next day. When I find old ones during the occasional clear out they make amusing reading, but are good for screwing up and getting the fire started. Anyway here are a few lists, or rather comments on things I like or don't.

Ten things I miss about England

1. Proper Fish and Chips, preferably wrapped in paper and from a good local chip shop, so everything is fresh. The ability to add my own amounts of salt and vinegar instead of the measly things you get pre salted in places like Mac... sorry can't even type the word without feeling ill.

2. Being able to buy my size shoes have always been a problem, but over here it's almost an impossibility, unless you go to the city. Size 13 is a 48; if I go into a shoe shop and ask for anything, and I mean anything in size 48 the assistants normally hold their breath in order not to start giggling. After apologising that they have nothing they watch me leaving whilst smirking at each other and gesticulating in the direction of my feet.

3. I have to admit that it was only on the rare occasion in Britain that I stood under spreading oak trees in green fields, whilst watching cows grazing contentedly. In the hazy blue distance, smoke could be seen rising from the chimneys of a local village and the spire of a distant cathedral could be seen on the skyline. Ok, a bit over the top but, better than the bunch of scrawny fly blown goats that have just passed outside.

4. A BIG FRIED BREAKFAST SERVED IN A STEAMY TRANSPORT CAFÉ, WITH A GIANT MUG OF TEA. Preferably, whilst it's raining outside. My friend back home tells me they are fast disappearing,

replaced by motorway facilities of the fast food variety. A couple of local bars have made a valiant effort to reproduce something similar over here, but they are still having problems with toast and you can forget Spanish tea bags and runny under-fried eggs.

5. Live music, decent cinema and a theatre that puts on understandable plays are all in short supply in this part of the woods. I am sure the coastal resorts have more to offer, but no way do I want to live in mini Britain. There are several choirs in the area, but as they generally wear bright red lipstick, tight flamenco dresses and carry large fans, I don't think it would quite suit my image; anyway I can't hit those high notes, not without help anyway.

6. I'm not a big drinker, but do miss a good British pub. Especially the type that have retained lots of wood, brass, and brewery traditions. Preferably a Good Beer Guide recommended pub, with a variety of real ale, a roaring fire and hushed conversations. Sorry but tiled Spanish bars, two big screens showing Barcelona verses Madrid for the fifth time this year, fizzy cold lager (it isn't beer) and all the locals apparently shouting at each other, does not float my boat. No amount of tapas can improve that. Anyway it isn't free any more.

7. Family, yes I do love them a lot, miss seeing them more regularly, but my life is here and they are always very welcome. I don't have a great deal of time left, if it's a case of staying here in the sun or moving back to grey damp Britain, then it's no contest. Mind you after Brexit, we may get kicked out anyway, Ho Hum!

8. Understanding what people are saying. I know it's my fault for being slow or lazy at learning the language. I can cope on a basic level, but it would be so much better especially in important situations like hospitals, police stations and at my lawyers, if I knew exactly what they were getting at, rather than a rough approximation. At least back home I could argue my case with any officious bugger in an office.

9. The ability to work for yourself legally, paying any tax owed

from your profits. It gave you a chance to follow what you liked doing. There is a saying that goes "Work at what you like and you will never be actually working" well something like that anyway. The trouble over here is that apart from doing the local car boot or the occasional private sale, to work for yourself requires registering and paying at least a couple of hundred euro a month. That's not very good if you make homemade cards for sale at a euro a pop.

10. Now I'm having trouble, can't actually think of anything else I miss about England. So I will leave it there unless I think of something later.

Things I don't miss about England

1. Let's get it out of the way first. Yep! The weather. I've been away so long now that I have built up a fantasy image that it was always cloudy and raining, or at least grey or foggy. I'm sure it's not that bad, and I do seem to remember sunny summer days when I was a kid. But then we didn't care what it was like as long as we could run around and get into trouble with our friends. On my few returns it has always been nondescript, as if the day was waiting for some action one way or another. That was all except the time I took a Spanish friend to London for a week. I told her to bring warm clothing, but it turned out to be a freak of a week, and the warmest of the year. We spent more time in Primark buying sweat shirts, than seeing the sites.

2. Neighbours

Actually they were not all bad, but in general, the number of people you actually knew in your road was limited to just a few. The ones who you knew the names of and were actually friendly enough to say hello and exchange a few words, were even less.

3. The work ethic

I suppose now that I am retired, my opinion is a bit clouded by the fact that I can get away without working, because I have some sort of pension. However, I have always thought that spending the best years of your life flogging away at a job, was a total waste of our time on this planet. Yes I know! We need the money. But getting up before it is even light, driving on crowded roads to an office or factory to spend eight or so hours scribbling nonsense or pushing levers, are we all mad? Even if you misguidedly think you are important, after we have gone somebody else does the job and we are forgotten. If you have, or had, a job you genuinely enjoy or enjoyed, then you are either lucky or a very smart person to have made the right decisions. I am well aware that many people desperately want a job to pay the bills and survive, but they can't find one. Life blackmails us all into having to work to survive, and I sympathise. I am talking here about the dispiriting fact that we are all bound to servitude no matter what.

4. Having mild depression most of my life, it is really hard to live amongst so many other people suffering the same. Britain as a whole seems to be wallowing in this malady as a nation. At least here you feel that despite knowing that the Spanish economy is going to the wall like many other nations, they don't feel the need to wallow in depression. Let's just have another fiesta. I am not talking here about individuals, but general mass perceptions or am I wrong on this, but then I'm wrong on most things, Ha!

5. The cost of living

It was hard to keep up with the cost of living in Britain. No matter what you earn, it always seemed just not quite enough. When I first came out here it was like nirvana, my council tax for a year was less than I was paying a month in England. Just about everything was cheaper. This has gradually changed and parity is fast approaching, but I hope we have a few more years yet where we feel we are still getting away with it.

6. Sorry to say it but teenagers, especially groups of them, at weekends hanging around, especially those in hoodies trying to look hard. Even the ones, who were just out for a good time at the weekend, in the pubs and clubs in town. On Friday and Saturday nights you had to weave your way through crowds of them

occupying most of the street, celebrating the drinking culture that we are now so famous for across Europe.

7. General violence, or at least the threat and reportage of it in newspapers. Here I only read the free papers, which is more about local events and the surprising interest in local political celebrities. The latest face that will stop Spain being corrupt.

8. Traffic! Everywhere in England. Sometimes you just feel like a processional caterpillar, nose to tail in endless lines. At least where I live it is thankfully different. I get one car pass my home about every fifteen minutes, enough said. At least around here I am not going to die from carbon monoxide poisoning, although I may get gored by a wild pig.

Ten things you didn't know about Spain

1. Spain supposedly invented the mop; I don't know how we prove that and likewise the beret. They are also responsible for that sticky blob on the end of a stick called Chupa Chups!

2. Juan Mica claims that his family were the first to invent a drink, called Nuez de Kola Coca', which he then took to the US and sold the recipe.

3. The Spanish, or more accurately those from Cadiz claim that they invented fried fish and chips. In the 18th century, Britain negotiated with this region, and it is believed that the English took the idea of fish 'n' chips back with them.

4. Apparently Spain is the only Country in Europe that produces bananas.

5. The Spanish create what they term Bellens at Christmas time. You see them all over the place from people's gardens to supermarkets. They are nativity scenes with model buildings, people and animals.

6. There's a Facebook group called "I worship Rafael Nadal's biceps"

7. The population of Madrid is just over 6 million, which is apparently more than the population of some Countries, such as Norway, Ireland, Scotland, and Denmark.

8. Christopher Columbus was apparently Italian. He had an agreement with the Spanish Catholic Monarchs, that he would be governor of any new lands he found for Spain. Needless to say they didn't keep the bargain.

9. When the Carthaginians invaded in 300 BCE, they called it Ispania, which meant "land of the rabbits". The Romans called it Hispania, which gradually changed to España. So essentially, Spain is the "land of rabbits"!

10. With 410 million native speakers, Spanish is the second most popular language in the world. Spanish is expected to be the first language of 50% of the population of the United States within 50 years. It is the official language of Spain and (hold your breath) Argentina, Bolivia, Colombia, Chile, Paraguay, Panama, Mexico, Nicaragua, Honduras, Guatemala, El Salvador, Ecuador, Cuba, Dominican Republic, Peru, Uruguay, Puerto Rico, Venezuela, and Equatorial Guinea.

More

Though Spain is more famous for its Red wine than white, the majority of its vineyards have white grapes

Spain is the number one producer of olive oil in the world with 44% of the world's olive oil production. That is more than twice that of Italy and four times that of Greece.

Spain has the lowest population density in Western Europe (excluding Scandinavia)

The North African inhabitants who first crossed the Straits of Gibraltar called it Iberia, which meant land of rivers ('Iber' meant river). When the Greeks invaded the peninsula, they called it

Hesperia, meaning "land of the setting sun" (since it was then the westernmost point of the European continent).

Spaniards celebrate the New Year by eating one grape with their family for each bell strike of the clock (for a total of 12 grapes – hence the name). This custom was originally popularized by Spanish vine growers as a way to sell their excess grapes!

The first surname of Spanish people is that of their father, the second could be their mother.

Ten things I promise never to do again

1   Buy anything from a cheap Chinese euro shop, except for fertilizer and plastic containers. But never again light bulbs, batteries, dog nail clippers, wasp spray, underpants and socks or any other of a dozen items that literally break after first usage, wear out, or shrink to infinitesimal size, or just plain never worked in the first place.

2. Use Entero milk, cheap teabags and saccharine tabs in my tea. One of my most treasured moments is to sit down with a nice cup of hot sugary tea, Ah bliss! Anything less than perfect and I instantly plunge into deep disappointment.

3. Wait in a queue whilst the shop assistant discusses babies with the person in front of me. Particularly, when the new born brat is screaming and trying to pull my bag of frozen beans off the counter.

4. Take in any more stray abandoned dogs. (I firmly say that now, but they only have to look at me with those eyes.)

5 Buy what looks like yummy Spanish cakes only to find out they are made of sawdust and polyfiller.

5 Mix with neighbours, who all they can do is grumble about Spain. Oh bugger! That means me as well.

6. Let a local Spanish plumber convince me that plastic fittings that were probably made in Korea are good and watertight. Their parting comment was "A few little leaks are to be expected." Even the woman in the shop did not want to sell me P.T.F.A tape as she said it would not be needed, HA!

7. Drive five extra kilometres just to buy petrol that is four cents cheaper and probably thinned down. Nobody can work out the self-service machine, so they still have to employ somebody to work it for you.

8. Expect any courier service to take the trouble to find out where I live, before sending my goods back to Britain or America.

9. Sign on with a dentist that only opens two days a week.

10. Try to amuse the policeman with my little bag of used breath test mouth pieces, suggesting he does not need to give me a new one.

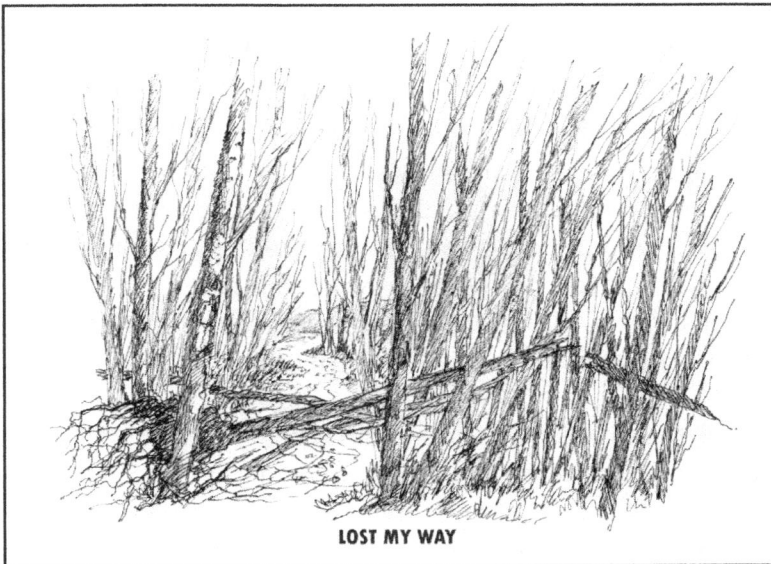

LOST MY WAY

POLITICAL HISTORY

There is no ignoring that Franco was a dictator who sanctioned some terrible things during Spain's civil war. But the (almost) united modern Spain of today is also a direct consequence of his actions. There were two distinct sides The Nationalist party was made up of monarchists, landowners, employers, the Roman Catholic Church and the army. Opposing them was the Republicans, who represented the workers, trade unions, idealistic socialists, and the rural peasant communities. The Country at that time was going through a rough economic period, even the American Wall Street crash had economic repercussions for them. By 1929 the military that had ruled Spain since 1923 collapsed, in its place came the elected Second Republic. These Republicans passed measures that reduced the power of the elites. In 1931 the King abdicated under the pressure they imposed. During the next few years there were periods when both political sides had a degree of control as the elected government. But violence, political killings and disorder were increasing from both sides. In 1935 Franco became army Chief of Staff, but was then banished to a remote post in the Canary Islands. When the military conspiracy first started taking shape, Franco was actually against it, but then changed his mind and became committed. In 1936 the army forcibly removed the Republicans from power, and Civil war ensued. It's a bit chilling to think that at the time of writing this, Spain is once again uttering threats of moving in the army to recalcitrant regions. They are a very volatile people under the veneer of calm.

Hitler and Mussolini both provided troops and equipment to aid the Nationalist side. France and Britain did not want Spain to fall to the Nationalists, as this would increase the control of the Fascist alliance of Germany and Italy. But they did not also want Spain to fall to the Republicans, who were Soviet-backed. There was a very real fear of Communism taking over the World. In the end they agreed on a form of non-intervention with the hope of blocking International aid. Russia sent aid to the Republicans, but was never as committed as Germany or Italy. Stalin had his own agenda, the

Russian leader, sold only enough supplies to the Republicans to keep them fighting. He was content that Germany was being kept busy with Spain, rather than concentrating its efforts in Eastern Europe. Young people in particular were fascinated by the idealism of fighting for the so called 'down trodden masses'. They flocked to help in large numbers from all over the World. It resulted in an International Brigade being formed from these idealists, socialists and communists, at times there were was many as 15,000 people fighting in these brigades, many of them British. However it was inevitable that the Nationalists would win and Madrid fell to them in 1939.

Franco who had earlier become, at the age of 33, the youngest General in all of Europe, ruled over Spain from 1939 until his death in 1975. Using the title of "El Caudillo" (The Leader), he persecuted political opponents, dissolved all other political parties, enforced the Spanish language on the Basque and Catalan regions, controlled the media and held absolute control over the Country, mainly by fear and the use of the army, particularly the Guardia. The Guardia are still treated with suspicion and some contempt to this day. Tribunals sent thousands of Spaniards to their death and at one time 26,000 political prisoners were being detained. In his later years there was a slackening of censorship and even some free market reforms took place. Surprisingly upon his death on 20 November 1975 he had chosen Prince Juan Carlos, the grandson of King Alfonso XIII, for the re-introduction of the monarchy, as he felt it was the best resolution for democracy. The first post-Franco elections were held in June 1977. The last judicial executions in Spain took place in September 1975 when three members of ETA and two members of FRAP were shot by firing squad. Three years later, the death penalty was banned. However, the clause banning capital punishment ended with a get-out clause for the Military.

YOUR STORIES, part 3

From Kay

Anyone who can tell their doctor that that she doesn't trust him because he could not even keep the dead pot plant on his window sill alive, is ok in my book. My friend Kay who I have known for years is one of those people that face the world full on; she says what she thinks without fear or favour. Everyone has down times, but she always appears full of humour, energy and remarkable ingenuity when it comes to fixing wangling, or downright deceiving the Authorities. She often says and does what the rest of us would like to say or do, but haven't the nerve. With her permission here are a couple of incidents that had me in stitches.

Kay is in that age group where we get bus passes, so planning ahead she cut out the medication info that she has to take and slipped them in the bus pass wallet. This made sense; at least if she was run over by the bus that didn't see her waving, they would look in it for her name and address and would see what medication she was on. But that was not enough, so Kay slipped in several packets of condoms, in her own words it was so "it would look like she still had an interesting life". One day she suddenly had a serious nose bleed, it did not stop for several hours and finally she got her son to take her to hospital. She walked in and was rushed into a curtained area and again in her own words "they shoved two inflatable tampons up my nostrils." Immediately her son took a picture and, I believe put it up on Facebook. But Kay got her own back and made him go bright red with embarrassment when the doctor pulled out his mums bus pass and littered the bed with Condoms. Apparently previous to this the chemist was having a sale and she didn't see any reason not to buy a large box of them at the discount price, most of them are now apparently out of date.

That reminds me of years ago seeing a programme hosted by Esther Ransom, where they investigated complains. Apparently a lot of young children had been very disappointed when their giant coloured balloons were found to be perished, and they deflated rather quickly. She found out that the company only produced two products, and you can guess what the other one was.

At the time of writing this it has been the craze for young men to grow extremely large square shaped beards, which mimic the traditional Muslim appearance. I have seen a lot of high profile footballers with them, must be a bit ticklish when you go up to head a ball together. Anyway, Kay was downtown shopping and spotted her son who had followed this trend. Coming up from behind she gave him a punch and demanded a hug, yes you guessed it, it wasn't him.

On another occasion she asked the car salesman in all seriousness that if she coughed and released a little bit of wee, when sitting on the electrically heated seats of the car she wanted to buy, would she electrocute herself.

From Me

Several years back I would sing in a local bar every Friday night, realising that the police would be bound to be on the lookout for anyone leaving a bar late I never drank much, if any, alcohol. Shortly after, I had an operation to fit a false knee and was soon after stopped and breath tested as expected. However, it proved negative, but the policeman did not think it was working properly, because I was staggering out of the car with my bad leg. He had seen me leave the bar and come to a conclusion I was drunk, and driving. He called in another police car and used their equipment to test me again, it also proved negative. Then they made me walk down the central line of the road, despite a couple of cars passing close by. Naturally I was not able to keep a straight line, but wobbled about either side of it. I think they wanted to take me down to the Station and give me a blood test or something so, in the end, I pulled up my trouser leg and showed them the livid scar where the week before I had over 50 metal staples embedded. After that they muttered a bit but had little option but to let me go. A week later I came out of the bar at a similar time and was pulled over again, staggering out of the car I could see the new policeman was savouring the moment, but his mate shouted from their car, something about "it's him" and with a disappointed shrug the officer waved me on my way.

From Jackie

Jackie used to help with a charity in Gibraltar, one Xmas Eve they got an urgent phone call from them. Two turkeys had been tied up alive on a sixth floor balcony. Would it be possible to smuggle them through the border to available land. Jackie had a big skirt; the turkeys were put on the passenger side under the skirt. (Jackie did not say if she was actually wearing it at the time.) Sometimes the Guardia would check, but this time they were lucky and the turkeys went home for Christmas with vegetarians. One didn't live long, but the other did, and was named Cranberry.

Another time they we were in a small village in the mountains and went for coffee and something to eat. The waiter brought great big rolls with cheese. For some reason Jackie turned hers over and spotted lots of little black specs, after close examination she realised they were ants baked in. The waiter was called, but he insisted that the bread was integral, and did not offer an apology even when confronted with the truth, he just asked if they would like another one, they declined.

From Jacqueline

I was in my shop when my son aged about 11 came running in shouting my uncle (who had been with them fishing) was dead. We ran out, but the port area was quite a way, so I stopped an old Spaniard on a moped explained and jumped on the back. By now there was half the town's women running behind my upset son, and an ambulance behind us. My uncle had slipped on rocks and was drifting out to sea, it was like a black comedy, but eventually he was rescued and ok.

An acquaintance of mine when I lived in the mountains, resided up the hill from the village and no other house overlooked his back garden. One day he thought that he would do a bit of naked sunbathing. All was fine and he drifted off to sleep. A loud cough woke him up, and he saw a friend on the track above his garden grinning down at him. After a wry comment or two, his friend said he had been following the foot procession on their way up the track to the local cemetery. So, at least fifty people had needed to avert their eyes, as they walked behind the coffin. My acquaintance thought it was a windup because he hadn't heard anything. But then the rockets started being let off up near the graveyard. It was traditional to let them off over the period of the silent procession, but obviously they had refrained as they passed, in honour of the naked sleeper.

From Joanne A friend's son, offered help in wiring some of their out-dated sockets in the cortijo they had just purchased. After completing the task, they plugged the TV in and settled back. She pressed the TV remote control, and the room lights came on.

Exposed Olive tree roots

IS IT JUST ME ?

The second hand shop had several wood doors and their frames stacked against the far wall, which had been ripped out of building reforms. To one side were several odd lengths that did not go with any complete set. There was a single 3 meter length of 2x2 which I asked if I could buy. "No it is part of a door frame" I was told. "Ok can I buy the complete door frame and if necessary the door as well?" No we don't have the other parts."

"Are you likely to get other matching parts?"

"No,"

"Ok then why can't I buy this part, as it's on its own?"

"Because it's part of a door frame. "

"Part of a door frame, you don't have, and won't be getting !"

"Yes"

At that point I gave up.

Here is a bit of Spanish logic. Jackie kept keys to loads of properties where they lived. Clive her husband did maintenance on them for holiday lets. One morning he did his rounds and one or more of them didn't have any water. This was strange because the rich German neighbour paid for a pump and it was pumped up from the lake so they never had to pay water bills. He went to explain that they had no water and that they can't have been cut off because there were no meters. The Secretary in the town hall said, "Buy meters and put them in and next time you have no water you'll know you've been cut off because you haven't paid the bills."

I went into a hardware shop that sold 20kl sacks of dry dog food.

"Can I have that one please?"

"No, that's our last one, which is our display bag, to show people what we sell.

"But you aren't selling any, when will you be getting more in?"

"We have stopped selling this brand."

"So why don't you sell me the last one?"

Because, it's our display bag."

Do you mean there is no dog food in it?"

No, it's full."

"So you won't sell me the last bag of a product that you are advertising, but will not be continuing with?"

At that point I realise I had been in this situation before, and left.

My friend wanted the TV in the window. He asked for it but was told it was just for display. He asked if they had any more, but they said no, so he asked again if he could buy it. They told him it did not have a box to go in. He said that was alright just stick it in any old box as long as the guarantee is ok. The man goes away and then returns with his manager's message that they can't sell it. So my friend said why put it in the window and stick a price on it, if you can't sell it and don't have any similar ones in your storeroom. The conversation went back and forth for some time and getting more heated before finally they agreed to sell my friend the TV and went looking for a suitable box. At that point my friend left the shop.

Another friend wanted to buy a new cooker. He pointed to the one on display and said he would like one of those. My friend asked if they were new, or was this particular one reduced as a display model. He was told that they were all brand new. The shop assistant said he would pack the cooker up for him.

"No, if they are all brand new I want a new one, still in its packaging.

"But Sir this one is new."

"No it's not, it's on display, People have been pushing its buttons and turning its knobs, I can see lots of finger marks on the chrome bits. If it's not reduced, but full price, then I want one in its packaging."

"Sorry we haven't got any."

From Pete J   Reminds of when I had to order a new router from Telefonica. Phoned them and placed an order, after two weeks it hadn't arrived so I phoned them again, three weeks later two brand new routers turned up. I phoned them and said I only ordered one but you have sent two. They said he could return one, where to I said, I don't know was the response I don't deal with returns, who does, the returns department, what's their number, I don't know we don't deal with them. On the next bill I was charged for two routers. I phoned up to complain and pointed out I only ordered one router and you have billed me for two, Yes because we sent you two, I pointed out that the first order didn't arrive so I phoned you to point that out, Yes she said that's why we sent you another one which makes two. I reminded her that I only phoned the second time because the first one hadn't arrived, but it has now so you have two and you must pay for both as you ordered a second one. That's when I gave up.

FROM SHEREE   A friend got a parking ticket from Granada when he wasn't even there, and he proved that he was at work in Malaga. But they said "we don't care prove you weren't in Granada?"

FROM ME The local council have just tarmacked a road that runs past my door, all very fine but it leads to a dead end, which just a small number of people use. Leading off it at the start are two dirt tracks that have a lot of nasty potholes, but which many people use on a constant basis to get to the main town of Baza, or a large village in the other direction. There are no plans to update these tracks.

From Pete C   I went into the bank to pay a bill (Tuesdays & Thursdays only between 8.30 & 10.30). Arrived just before 10am bank was crowded with other customer wanting to pay bills, finally got to the counter at 10.40 told you owe an extra 3 euro for late payment. I said, but I was here before 10, "yes" teller said but, you didn't get to the counter until after 10.30. I said, "Why doesn't your colleague help to speed things up?" Answer, my colleague is on breakfast break from 10 to 10.30 so only me serving.

I also spoke to farmer friend about 7 pm during Olive picking season, asked him why they didn't work all through the day time like in UK instead of stopping for 2 -3 hours in the afternoon for siesta then coming back out at night to work in the dark. Answer was, because siesta is always in the afternoon.

From Wesley Try getting a NIE in Palma ...
Yo: Buenas dias
Yo: estoy buscando asignacion de NIE por favor, mas no hablo mucho Español.
Oficial de Oficina: "No preocupa se porque yo hablo mucho español!"

Me: good morning, I am looking for an NIE allowance pleas, but I don't speak much Spanish.

Officer Estranhero? " don't worry about it because I speak a lot of Spanish!"

MORE IS IT JUST ME

The number plate of a car seems to reflect the driver, or is that just my imagination. Nearly run off the road by a speeding van going down the middle of the lane, the plate was FYM (fuck you mate), or the very slow old car dawdling down the same lane completely oblivious to three cars behind him JHN (just having a nap). And the rusty old heap with BMW (Wishful thinking or a good joke)

I have a problem with supermarkets, I always seem to be stalking somebody, usually female, and honestly it's not intentional. It normally starts when picking up a trolley from the rack outside at the same time, so I politely let them go first. Then a minute or so later we are both reaching for the same product. After somehow following each other down a couple of isles, I realise that we are bound on the same course around the supermarket, so as by now I'm feeling a little bit uncomfortable about our regular encounters. I turn around and head for a different route only to find them doing the same. It doesn't matter how many detours I make it keeps happening, to the extent that I go and stand examining the fish or veg counter for five minutes, hoping that they have finished and gone. But low and behold when I finally get to the pay-out guess who is usually within sight. If I am really unlucky we are both trying to exit the car park at the same moment, God forbid I am heading down the road in the same direction trailing them. Now this has happened several times with different random people, is it just me?

I BELIEVE

I have believed ever since entering Spain, that no two offices in the local councils know what the other is doing. This is surprising seeing as how they are often related (not related by topic, I mean related by family ties.) It's definitely a case of jobs for the boys and girls. Spain has among the most stifling (and over-staffed) bureaucracy in Western Europe (even worse than the French!) and any encounter with officialdom is a test of endurance and patience. Official offices (if you can find the right one) often open only for a few hours on certain days of the week; the person dealing with your case is always absent; you never have the right papers (or your papers and files have disappeared altogether); the rules and regulations have changed (again). Official inefficiency has been developed to a fine art in Spain. Officialdom is generally disorganised and the only predictable thing about them is their unpredictability. Spain has been described as part advanced high-tech nation and part banana republic, where nothing quite works as it should. And deadlines are treated with a degree of disdain. This morning I was almost arrested, well that was according to my friend who was with me and speaks good Spanish. As for me I was just putting my right to free speech to the test. But it is a good example of the Spanish dogmatic nature clashing with their, 'what the hell,' approach.

A neighbour was having a dispute about land rights. Due to helping erect a fence three years ago I, therefore, got called up as a witness. The Draconian letter I received threatened that if I did not turn up at the appointed hour, measures would be taken. I found out that it could have taken the route of a few thousand euros in fines. Anyway, quite a time before it came to court, my neighbour declared that a solution had been found and the case would be cancelled, there was no need for me to go. Being very cautious and, as I just mentioned, with the knowledge that here at least the left hand did not always know what the right was doing. I decided, along with a friend who was also called up, to go there the day before and just check. The response was that we had to come the next day as arranged, even if it did not take place, and yes we could be fined if we didn't. So the following morning I arrived outside to see my friend talking to a casually dressed woman who was smoking a fag. I assumed it was a friend, but turned out to be the Clerk of the Court. Basically she just told us to piss off, there was no hearing. Unconvinced I asked her why we had not been informed and she said she had only heard yesterday. Now that's plain bollocks! I knew at least three weeks before, but the clerk of the court had only known yesterday? As we walked away I got a bit annoyed and went back, determined at least to get my paper stamped, to prove I had been there. After all I was still likely to receive a multa from the fines department, who would have no record of me signing in. After all the police had said that case or no case I had to attend or get fined. After a long animated discussion with the woman who was still smoking and more concerned that a traffic warden was about to put a sticker on her car (How dare he, I'm an important member of the Council), she basically refused to sign or stamp my paper. The two guards had their hands resting on their holsters and my friend was hovering at the door beckoning me away. Things got to an impasse as I refused to leave. Finally an old policeman, who was way past retirement age, beckoned me over and signed the back of my letter. Like I said they are both casual and bureaucratic, often at the same time, which is no mean feat.

YOUR STORIES , part 4

From Jackie

A couple of years ago friends found a Pointer roaming around the boot sale in Baza and felt he was meant for them. So they took him home had his jabs done, and had him doctored. But one day he went missing, well! We looked everywhere and eventually got a phone call to say they thought he was being held in this derelict barn in Los Olivos, so we sneaked over there after dark. The dog was on a chain locked in this building, with no water, so we rescued it and hid it under blanket in back of car. Unfortunately despite it looking almost identical, it was a girl not a boy. We had to regretfully sneak it back.

We had our donkey 'Carrito' in a field below the Castle, but he was quite an escapologist. They used to use the Castle for making films, including Don Quixote featuring Bob Hoskins. The crew spent a whole night preparing the courtyard to be a medieval market, but when we got up to go to work, we heard all this shrieking, the donkey had got into the courtyard and scoffed all the food and done a good job on dismantling several stalls. We denied all knowledge and never said a word.

We had a big Sherpa van with Gibraltar plates, we used to park it at the Spanish side of the border and pay a stickman a bit of money every day to keep an eye on it. We gave him a bit of extra money one week to clean it, it was originally white but, but was not anymore, for when we got back, he said 'I've used a whole bottle of bleach on it.' The van eventually died, so we gave it to the stickman, because he lived in a little car. He stopped us one day and said 'the Guardia won't let me live in the van in the field cos it has Gibraltar plates.'

From Stephen

I was told if I could punch the bull on the nose at the local Bull Run I would get free alcohol for the year from this particular bar, plus a whole jamon. I obviously failed and got nailed by the said bull! Whilst recovering I was introduced to the local Guardia Sergeant who told me he knew I was going to get hit by the bull, to which I replied "That is why you are a Guardia Sergeant and I'm just a stupid Englishman!" He then introduced me to his boss the head of the Guardia for the whole of Granada. Much merriment followed including having to sing a song with my teenage son to a packed bar of Spaniards before we were allowed a drink. We were driven back to my house by the police and my wife arriving at the front door in her PJs and being confronted by in her words, three drop dead gorgeous policemen. They made a fuss of my St Bernard and played Dire Straits CDs until about 6am

From Fenella

My mum tried practising her Spanish on our old neighbour. She had nearly finished decorating the lounge and said I only need a few cojones instead of cojines. Our neighbours face was a picture and she burst into laughter before explaining to what she had said.

From Tom

We found that our log burner did not draw very well, and we were struggling to build a good fire. So in my wisdom I decided to pour quite a lot of fire lighting fluid on to a smouldering fire. I stood back admiring my handy work, and the fire starting to build when 'Bang' an enormous explosion occurred. The log burner's glass door shattered and exploded into the lounge with me standing a few feet away. I was covered in glass and in total shock. My first thought was OMG my tackle, is it still there? And yes it was all ok, but I had cuts to my hands and face, but nothing serious, the dogs were in shock and shaking but my wife was calm and sorted us all out. We proceeded to then clear up, the room was covered in glass and bits of burnt wood, smoke was everywhere, we had only just decorated the whole room. What a mess, lesson learned. The general problem had been that whoever had fitted the flue pipes had put them in upside down. We had been getting black thick watery slick running down inside and the pipes were rotten with holes, right through the chimney , I had to demolish a ten foot high stack ,replace all pipes and rebuild, all whilst it was an extremely cold February.

Yet another small mishap. We decided to build a small porch to the front of our cave, nothing elaborate just a wooden roof structure, covered against the sun. I started to build my porch, putting a support beam all around walls and hanging roof struts off of them, I needed to use a step ladder to reach about 9 foot high. I was on the ladder drilling and screwing the beams together, when I twisted around and lost my balance , the step ladder fell from under me and left me hanging on my roof struts , which unfortunately were not designed to support my weight. The roof and I descended to the ground completely wrecked; I had not put the ladder locks on.

Recently I was helping at the local dog sanctuary. Due to a slight lapse of concentration, I put two quite big strong dogs in the same pen; they naturally proceeded to tear each other apart. I dived in to smother one, whose jaws could have easily locked on the other. Unfortunately that gave the second dog free reign to take it out on my hands. During the confusion with several other dogs joining in the melee, my friend attempted to pull me out of the pen by one leg, I am not sure it helped much, but somehow we managed to separate them. My only reward for my heroic act was a visit to the local hospital, with punctured hands.

More from Pop

I'd always enjoyed cycling but apart from the London to Brighton ride in 1988, and a few cycling holidays in the early 70s, I'd never done any long distances, so when flying back from a holiday on the Costa Blanca I looked out of the plane at the many small roads winding across Spain, and thought 'I'd love to ride a bike across there' I thought it would remain a dream. But a few weeks later my friend Bob and I had gone for one of our regular strolls around the local inns (OK, a pub crawl) and I mentioned at the end of the evening that I'd thought it would be fun to cycle across Spain he immediately said 'Yesh, letsh do it'. So the next day I gave up smoking and alcohol and pretty well every evening we'd go on a 20 or 30 mile bike ride, or spend an hour in the nearby gym. I lost stones in weight, and became fitter than I ever had been - I was 42 by now. We did this for nearly a year before boarding the ferry at Plymouth and had a smooth crossing to Santander where we jumped on our bikes and set off for Javea, 660 klms away. We'd gone about 60 kilometres, when we hit the road that wound up to the Spanish plateau, a steep, windy Alpine type climb that we undertook in bottom gear and very slowly. This was to be a 12 km ascent but halfway up there was a café bar where we decided to stop for a coffee and a very crusty cheese bocadillo. I'll digress, if I may...in my late teens I had an abscess behind my top front teeth, my dentist did what he could but eventually I had 4 teeth removed and replaced with a plastic bridge, which worked fine apart from the fact I couldn't eat toffee. So I was hungrily biting into my cheese bocadillo when there was a loud crack - the plastic bridge which held my front teeth had split down the middle! Now, I'll admit I'm not one to be over fussed about my appearance but I didn't fancy crossing Spain looking like Nobby Stiles in '66, but where was I going to find a dentist who could repair a bridge in a day? Luckily Bob remembered my young cousin Christina showing him some craft work she was doing when we were both in Spain a couple of years earlier and she'd told him superglue in Spanish was Super pergamento, so we stopped at the next town, found a likely looking shop and bought a tube, then sat on a bench while I glued my teeth back together. It did the trick, though I had to glue them back together a couple of more times on the trip, a journey which went well and we completed in 5 days, an average of 110 klms a day.

From Friends

While we were on this campsite by Algeciras a man had to return to England on urgent business. He owned a very expensive motorhome and gave us permission to camp in his posh awning if we looked after his dogs and that he would pay us. The awning was loads bigger than our tent so we readily agreed. He had hardly gone, when the heavens opened and the campsite was flooded by a huge deluge. The dogs were fine and cosy in the motorhome and looking out of the window at us as we suffered in a leaky awning, god knows what condition our tent was in. If that was not bad enough, my husband and I spent the night in our damp camp beds, whacking rats with bamboo sticks. Apparently the old building next to the site was riddled with them. Once the water flooded it, they sought dryer ground.

True Snippets

Friends in Spain found two rams horns in almost perfect condition, on an old carcass. Their two small dogs tried to drag them home. After cleaning them, the lady put them on display with two candles sticking out of them. It was only after someone remarked that their living room looked like Satan's coven that they realised that black candles in ram's horns rather gave the wrong impression.

Two friends who went back to England were invited to a fancy dress party. Having little with them they went to a costume hire shop and for some reason he hired a monkey suit. They were watching television the night before and he had hung the costumes on hooks on the door behind them. Some movement made his wife turn around, she shot out of the seat with a scream, saying the monkey was alive; its leg was swinging backwards and forwards. Turns out the cat had got inside, and then panicked.

An old guy, who was walking through the Spanish village I used to live in, needed to pee rather quickly but unfortunately he was in the high street. Seeking any corner where he could be somewhat inconspicuous, he leaned over a low railing that overlooked a narrow passage behind houses. At some embarrassing point a back door opened and the local priest walked out. According to the old man, who later told his tale in the local bar, the priest genuflected said go in peace, smiled and walked away. I don't know if the double meaning is the same in Spanish and English, but after the discomfort of a full bladder, going in peace is certainly very apt. Anyway his mates thought it was funny.

A lady friend told me this one.

When I first came to Spain, I had a hire car for a couple of weeks. Driving carefully and still not completely used to driving on the right, I went the wrong way round a roundabout. Luckily nothing was coming, but a guy behind me purposely accelerated and overtook me by going the right way round it. Then he slowed down and stopped, got out of his car came back to me and started ranting through my side window. Being in the wrong, I tried to apologies in my faltering Spanish, but it just seemed to get him angrier. By this time there were two more cars behind us, starting to sound their horns. He ignored the fact that he was now the one causing a problem and began to shout even louder and going red in the face, I guess he just didn't like the English. Finally he uttered a few obvious swear words and stormed back to his car, before accelerating away rapidly, even burning a bit of rubber. About a kilometre or so further on I passed him, he was standing looking at the dent in his front grill, where he had driven into a bollard. I could not repress a grin.

Peter is a friend and near neighbour who delights in fiddling with anything of a computer or electronic nature. He has an interest in gadgets especially if he can construct them from the thousands of components he has scattered in his candy store of a work room. Although I did catch him buying store shelves to put them all in, but we shall see. I have the same situation in my art room. (I could put stuff away logically, but everything prefers to just hang about wherever it wants.) Anyway what makes him different from others, who like fiddling with computers, is that he has an inventors mind. Repairing a computer or its programs is boring; he would rather construct a solution to a problem that often ends up rather more amusing. I've mentioned Pete in my previous book where he constructed a device in the hall of his ageing mother in England so he could keep an eye on her from his home in Spain. It registered every time she passed by and issued a friendly greeting. Since then he decided that his home needed protection, so up went a camera, but the only people he caught was an old lady who nicked some of his wild roses, and me pulling faces at him. However, that was not enough so he created a barking dog; unfortunately the initial pitch was more like a frustrated Chihuahua. But undaunted he just adjusted it down through the pitches till it sounded like an altogether different and slightly angry breed. Out here in the campo he was more likely to get a concerned neighbour breaking in to rescue the animal because its owner had shut it in and gone away. Last week I went around for a coffee or was it a beer, probably both. My friend suddenly started collecting fruit and a single tomato (is that a fruit or vegetable?) just one of each of an assortment was laid in front of me. If I remember there was a banana, avocado, orange, peach, lemon and something else. Then out came a laptop and a whole series of wires. He plugged a wire into each fruit, and then proceeded to play them like drums. Each item produced a different drum sound. If you don't believe me we have video proof, Ha!

He is now working on controlling his outside telescope by remote control. As we live miles from anyone and no discernible neighbours it will have to point at the stars instead at the lighted window of the blond at no 37. (My imagination at it again)

From June

We were strolling on a beach in bikinis when we reached a part that was obviously sectioned off as a nudist beach. Rather than turn back we stripped off and buried our costumes in the sand under a rock, then walked on up the beach. Unfortunately, when we returned we could not find our costumes. We could not leave the nudist part, because of lack of any attire. In the end we swam out to sea and made a curving approach to the area of the beach where our family was sunbathing. Making various gestures and waving without revealing anything we managed to attract the attention of one of our sons, who was on a floating canoe. But then he just shouted loudly to his dad on the beach that his mum had no clothes on. This apparently caused some laughter from other Brits sunbathing nearby. When we eventually exited the water, having been thrown some coverings, it was to a round of applause.

On another occasion June and her partner were, on a motorbike, touring. They reached a campsite quite late at night. Setting up the tent they retired for the night, intending to book in in the morning when the office would be open. Crawling out of their tent to find the shower block the next day they were confronted with the sight of a gentleman cycling past completely nude and clutching a long stick of bread. Yep! They had camped in a nudist colony.

June, who does not speak much Spanish, was trying to buy some eggs. When the shopkeeper did not understand her, she mimed a chicken. He went and got her a whole chicken. 'No, No' she said and began miming a chicken again, but this time squatting down and pointing at her backside. He went around the back and re-appeared with a toilet roll. My friend did her chicken act again plus pointing at her bum then pointing at her mouth, as if hungry. This completely floored him, till she started cracking imaginary eggs. By this time they were both crying with laughter.

From a friend An Alberca is a round concrete structure, often found in parts of rural Spain. It has high sided walls and no door. These are filled with enough water to irrigate the surrounding land. Most when full appear like reasonably large swimming pools. This is what one man decided he would do, so he stripped off and dived in an enjoyed a good swim. Unfortunately somebody opened the stop tap and hundreds of gallons of water quickly sped off down the large pipes to feed the olive and avocado plantations. Within minutes it was impossible for the man to reach up the smooth walls, and grasp the concrete rim, so he continued to keep afloat whilst the thing emptied. Finally he was standing in a foot or so of water looking up perhaps fifteen or more feet to the only way out, outlined against the sky. He apparently shouted for ages, but nobody heard him. His only option was to wait hours, or possibly even days, before it was filled up again so that he could rise with the water line. In these rural areas the amount of water from the local canals that can be used by any landowner is regulated. You are allowed so many days each month, so in theory he could have to wait a week or so. Like I said these Albercas are generally out in the countryside and not near property. Anyway luckily someone did eventually hear him and after much banter, a rope was found and lowered over the side.

A friend tried to by some gas jets to replace the ones he had in his cooker. They sold them at the gas showroom and were only a euro or so each. But the person would not sell them to him, he had to have an appointment for the guy to come out and replace them,(a matter of five minutes work) He wanted 50 euros for doing it, explaining that it needed a very special tool to do the job. My friend explained that he also had this tool, as he had just removed all the old ones; it was called a small spanner.

I always burn chicken. I don't cook it for myself it's just boiled with vegetables for the dogs healthy eating schedule, seeing as the vet said they were all too fat and the little one probably had an allergic reaction to tinned dog meat. So I stagger from the supermarket with two carrier bags full of dog and cat food and one tin of beans and six eggs for me. Anyway I stick a couple of chicken legs in a big pan of water, with a packet of frozen chopped runner beans or spinach and let it boil. The only trouble is its really boring waiting in the kitchen for it, so I go off and get involved in something else. Problem occurs almost every time, because I just forget. So usually the first sign is a sudden whiff of burning at which point I head off, normally from my computer which is at the far end of my cave system, and am usually greeted by a pall of smoke hanging in the air. By the time I make it to the stove and turn it off I usually have my shirt pulled up over my mouth to prevent inhalation of fumes. The remains of the chicken and beans are usually just a black burnt sludge at the bottom of the pan. Now if this happened just once in a blue moon it would be understandable, but it happens nearly every time, well at least once or even twice a week. On one occasion I even drove into the local town and went shopping, all that was left was a pan without a bottom, grey powder all over the gas ring which was still going, and a terrible odour of burnt chicken bone that took several days to clear. I seem to have a black hole in my brain when it comes to chicken. I should take an egg timer or alarm clock with me, but that requires planning and I keep forgetting to do that. It's all tied in with my dislike of cooking in general which I explained rather graphically in the first book. Just about anything is more interesting than cooking for me, even ironing, well no actually they are both very low on my list of things I want to spend my life doing.

A friend related the tale of a dog that always liked to pee on the vacuum cleaner, which was stored under the stairs. When they sorted that problem out they thought their troubles were over. Sometime later they began to notice the smell of urine in the living room. Dutifully cleaning under all the chair legs and banning the dog from the room, they hoped that had sorted the problem, but the smell grew worse. Finally they moved the large Moroccan tagine that was displayed under the dining table. They had already wiped it down but, as it was large, had not bothered to pull it out and look inside the big pointed cone of a lid. When they did they were greeted with the acrid smell of ancient pee and several inches of the liquid inside. Apparently the dog had been peeing on the cone lid and the liquid had been running down and seeping inside the rim. He must have been doing this for quite some time.

From Tom

The casa next door has been empty for five years. The property has been left to run down and needed lots of cleaning and reforming . One day walking up and down outside were a young couple, they told us they were the new owners of next door, so we started to chat about stuff and we asked where they were from. They explained it was from a small place we would not know in middle of UK, called 'Oundle'. That took me back a bit, as when we lived in England, we had lived 8 miles away. We then told them our surname, it turned out that they even knew three of our children due to school connections and later through work. Subsequently, we mucked in and helped clean the place up and later reformed it for them. On further discussion, my wife mentioned that her family originally came from Woodford. The man piped up that so did his, their families would have known each other as it was only a small community back then. I started telling them about my great grandfather who moved from Shennington Oxfordshire to Northampton and married a girl as she was with child. Unfortunately, my great granddad was married already, so he was a bigamist. The neighbour then said one of his ancestors was from a bigamist marriage In Northampton. "Oh no can't be, are we related?

Anywhere but here and now from John

Not long ago when I was on a course of antibiotics they always had a certain effect on me, just to say it was not wise to roam to far from the availability of a toilet. Unfortunately, on one trip across the campo I was given no notice and swerved off the road up a track and pulled to an abrupt halt in an olive grove. Without going into too many details, let's just say I wasn't quick enough. Disguarding garments into a handy carrier bag, I drove home naked from the waist down. Thank God it was the countryside and not in the centre of town.

However this episode reminded me of a couple that befell others. A man, who used to play in the same marching band as me in our local village, had a similar problem. One day as the band marched left down a side street he went straight on at a run and into the local pub. Unfortunately he plays the tuba which wedged on the toilet door causing him to panic. He threw it at the nearest table and dived for safety. I didn't dare ask if he made it, but he did show me the dent in his tuba, where it slid off the table and hit the floor.

Somebody told me about their cousin who was a best man at a wedding. Standing in front of the assembled guests he thought his humorous speech was going down well, because people were tittering, but apparently his wife was trying to signal him. He ignored her at first, until it was obvious she was trying to desperately get his attention. It turned out that his flies were open and his red underpants were caught in the zip. Later he explained that he had been so nervous that he had rushed to have a pee just before his speech and had not taken care in adjusting everything. The groom has a colour picture in their wedding album of the infamous speech.

From Anita A Spanish friend appeared one morning with two baby goats in the back of the car. I thought he had just come to show us, as he knows we love goats. He said goodbye and drove off with us shouting you have left the goats. He said they are yours, and they need feeding with a bottle every so many hours, and then he was gone.

Us being us, I bought a bottle and kept them. They were male and I now know they were not wanted, but we loved them. One of them got sick we took him to the vet and he had a fan club everyone taking his photo. He was sitting on my lap loving the attention.

He had disease young goats get if the umbilical cord gets infected. His back legs kept giving way so we put him in the wheelbarrow when we took them all out in the forest, 2 goats and 5 dogs. Unfortunately he died but his brother grew up to be the stingiest goat ever, but we loved him.

Ruined Arch, ornamental house feature

FOOD

After those last couple of distasteful comments, what about food?

An average family meal, Ha!

TAPAS

This is just the beginning, supposedly light nibbles, whilst everyone is arriving and getting comfortable. But to someone new to it, the amount can seem like a meal on its own, but they are easy to pre-prepare.

> Artichokes, sautéed with ham or filled with white sauce and meat.
> Gambas a la plancha (Pan-grilled shrimp)
> Spanish Chorizo on bread.
> Anything almost goes with anything in tappas.

PRIMER PLATO

Just getting going now, so what about one of the following?

Sopa de Pescado y Marisco or cold gazpacho.

Cocido soup could have any amount of different meats swimming in it.

There will most certainly be a very complex salad .

PLATO PRINCIPAL

This is the main course and likely to be beef, lamb, poultry or game and would be served with fried pan potatoes or possibly rice. Roast lamb is far less work than a turkey or duck and just as tasty. At a Spanish event, the amounts served would last most of us several days, and provide enough bones to keep the family pet happy for even longer.

POSTRE

You could take your pick from:

Spanish Crumble cakes (Mantecados) or almond candy (Turon), almond cookies (Polvorones), crème custard or rice pudding.

Plenty of red wine and cava, lots of lively discussions and laughter, followed by coffee, cheese, chocolate or anything that's left over.

The whole idea is to take your time and enjoy it along with good company.

Tapas: What to expect in Spain

You may have to be quick, things are changing but Granada is one of the few cities in Spain still serving tapas basically without payment, or as near as you are going to get to a free meal. Unfortunately, most of Spain has realised they can charge for it now. The name, 'tapa', comes from 'tapar', to cover. A popular belief is that when in the 13th-century King Alfonso became very ill, they prescribed small portions of food with his wine to help him recover. He enjoyed this form of snacking, and passed a law making bars serve food with the alcohol. Others suggest that a piece of bread was provided to place over the beer to keep the flies out, but people kept eating it.

There are bars of all styles from Andalusia-tiled interior covered in posters of bullfights and fiestas, to greasy spoon types, but the ones that serve good tapas are always rammed full with people, it's definitely standing room only, which is how the locals like it.

The Tapas will vary from bar to bar, it could be mouth-watering roast ham, Patatas a la Pobre (potatoes fried with onions and green peppers) and sometimes augmented with a quail's egg, sherry-soaked clams, fried aubergine in oil with garlic or drizzled in honey, fried salt cod , hot stew, chorizo kebabs or tortilla, to name but a few variations. Mind you -you may not fancy the Sacromonte omelette with lamb's brains. Many of them state on their menus that tapas are a gift, which means they decide what you get, normally you cannot choose. With each successive drink you should get offered different tapas.

If all you are accustomed to is a dubious bowl of peanuts on the counter in your local pub, tapas comes as a great and welcome surprise.

How to make the perfect Paella

Any dish that gains International recognition is going to get very quickly developed and altered according to whichever chef is attempting it. National and Regional tastes will vary, as will availability of certain produce. The paella has probably had more variations than most dishes and is not easy to cook perfectly. Starting with the basic rice, which in itself could be any number of varieties, what goes in after that can vary in the extreme. So how can we create perfect Paella? Well! A good starting point would be to look at its origins in Spain and the Valencia region in particular. They claim this dish as their birth right and it should only be cooked and eaten out of doors and on a wood fire, under an old tree and always during the middle of the day. They also sneer at using fish and shellfish, preferring chicken or rabbit, but quite like a few snails added as a treat.

That may be authentic, but basically impractical and possibly somewhat distasteful for most of us, so let's consider some alternatives. The seafood version, more to tourist's tastes, was developed on the coast, where its basic marine ingredients are plentiful.

Paella is, before anything else, a rice dish. You need to use a short grained variety that can easily absorb the liquid stock and not dry out. The best is Spanish *Bomba*; it forms a crisp base known as *Socarrat* that is considered one of the best bits of the paella. You obviously need a paella pan, one with a thin base, so that the liquids cook off evenly and relatively quickly. One thing you should never do is stir, this is not a risotto.

Don't have a wood fire?

Start the paella on the stove, but finish it off in the oven. Sautéing onion, peppers, a touch of paprika and some garlic, plus whatever fish or meat you desire, add the rice and heat for a couple of minutes before adding the stock. Now you can ramp up the heat, so everything simmers quite vigorously, for about ten minutes. Lastly add any seafood on the top, and leave to cook for a further eight or so minutes. Let it rest, with some aluminium foil over it, then serve hot, with lots of crusty bread and a good glass of wine.

LOST IN TRANSLATION

FROM KATE Whilst living and studying in Spain, I suggested to a Spanish friend that we sit down. Instead of vamos a sentarnos, I said vamos a sentirnos which apparently means "let's go and feel ourselves"

FROM PHIL A friend tried to impress me with their Spanish at a Spanish restaurant. With little appetite, he said No tengo hombre, quiero solo patatas fritas instead of No tengo hambre, quiero solo patatas fritas - the difference being 'I haven't got a man, I'd like just chips'

FROM ROGER Some friends were visiting from Argentina and during a picnic, I thought I would show their young son that I had a grip on Spanish. I kept asking him if he wanted zapatos fritos, and he just kept saying "¿Qué?" I thought the poor kid didn't have an idea what potato chips were ... ahem ... I found out later chips are patatas fritas, and I was offering him fried shoes.

When I went to Spain I knew very little Spanish. One day some friendly person tried to make conversation and I tried to tell him that I had only studied Spanish for one year. But I forgot all about the tilde and its effect on the pronunciation of the second letter in the word for "year" in Spanish. What I said was that I had studied Spanish for one ass. Another time I was having seafood paella, a loud woman on the tour was bragging that she knew the ingredients in the paella. She announced "These are testicles. The Spanish people love to eat octopus testicles!"

One of the common errors is the mix up between POLLO (chicken) and POLLA (cock/dick).

Somebody tells the story of when she first started going to Spain with her (then) husband. He knew the difference between the two words but she didn't and every night in the restaurant he would encourage her to order "polla con patatas fritas".Each evening, oblivious to the sniggering coming from both her husband and the waiter, she would proudly ask for her "cock and chips" On the last night of her stay, she once again ordered her usual from a smiling Spanish waiter and waited for her meal to arrive. Suddenly, all the waiters from the restaurant appeared at the table with a plate of chips with an enormous plastic Willy stuck bolt upright in the middle of it.

From a Spaniard visiting England.   Honestly don't know where I got this from;

"¿Qué vas a decirle, papá? asked Cynthia.

'I want a dick with cock.'"

What he meant was that he wanted a Whisky DYK, which is a well-known Spanish brand.

From Mowser
I asked the cal man how much limestone rock I should buy to paint my cave. He said about "dos arrobas."
Obviously I had to look it up and saw that an arroba was a unit of weight roughly 11.3 kg (25lbs). I went to a local shop and tried for the life of me to remember the word. My Spanish was really poor then. I kept getting confused with "quiero", "quisiera" and "tengo." Instead of saying "Quisiera dos arrobas de cal" (I would like two arrobas of limestone), I said "Tengo .... Almorranas." She looked at me and asked again. I said "almorranas." She told me to ask next door. I said the same phrase to the chemist who was next door; they produced creams and suppositories for piles!

(Arrobas, units of weight. Almorranas, haemorrhoids.)

From Clara I asked for a cheque for my landlady, the cashier looked at me askance and started pointing at his head, saying "Blanca, Blanca", apparently I was asking for a cheque for my dandruff!

From Tracey When Mum and Dad were first in Spain Dad always ordered everything in English but with an O at the end! Two- o-Beeros please? For some reason he thought that was ok?!

From Christine Whilst giving a statement to the police after having my handbag stolen I had to give details of what it contained. I said my Nationwide bank card. The police officer didn't understand and asked me to write it down. When he read it he said, "Ahhh.... NAT EON WIDY." It's been that ever since!

From Frances   Couple new to Spain told friends they had found a white plastic garden chair all on its own at side of road. Next trip to town found another one. In the end they managed to collect four this way. Proudly told friend only need to buy a White plastic table and would have a garden set. Imagine their faces when told whose chairs they had taken - the Ladies must have wondered where their chairs kept disappearing to.

From Dom Needed to buy a new car battery the guy in the shop ask what car it was, I told him he went off and never came back so after about 20 mins I left the shop not understanding until I found out Pajero meant Wanker/ Tosser which is why it's called a Galloper in Spain

From Ines I came out here as a kid's entertainer. I got asked to perform at a Spanish kids party, the Mum was English. I face painted, did the games and then performed my magic act. The piece de resistance was producing a rabbit at the end (no cruelty involved). Of course the kids wanted to stroke the rabbit and then after I would take the rabbit round for the parents. I said in my best Spanish to a gentleman 'Quieres tocar mi conejito' Conejo is rabbit, 'ito' on the end means small, hence would you like to stroke my small rabbit. The man said something like 'but my wife is here', whilst smiling and gesturing to his wife. I didn't understand, smiled back and repeated. Suddenly aware of everyone else laughing the English mum informed me Conejito means pussy.......they booked me again next year!

Over the years, my in-laws rented out a flat to students who attended various language schools in Malaga. Often they would invite all the students to lunch and one day a young lady, who was normally very quiet and polite, mentioned how hard she was finding it to remember all the vocabulary. Then, to stunned silence, she suddenly asked, "Me puedes explicar otra vez la diferencia entre cajón, cojín **y** cojón?"

My other half. said he wanted to thank the Spanish man for the firewood. I told him the word for wood; he went over to him and spoke. Pepe looked very surprised, smiled tentatively, nodded and shot indoors. I asked the neighbour what my husband had said, found out he'd only thanked Pepe for his 'mother'!

From a Spanish lady visiting Scotland, talking about the language mistakes she had made

I asked to my landlady for "shits" for my bed, I used to say that I lived in Alicante where there are very nice "bitches", of course I meant "beaches. To me the most hilarious one occurred when taking the speaking Cambridge exam with my classmate. He told to the examiner: "I don't want you to piss me off". Then I kicked him but he didn't realise... Having finished the exam he told me what he meant was: "I wouldn't like to bother you" I wonder who taught him that?

ESTOY CALIENTE I'm Hot baby **TENGO CALOR** I'm a bit warm.

This one from Mexico but at least it's a Spanish speaking country and too good to miss out.

When Parker Pen marketed a ball-point pen in Mexico, its ads were supposed to have read, *It won't leak in your pocket and embarrass you.* The company, thought that the word "embarazar" meant, "to embarrass" (which it didn't) so the ad said.

It won't leak in your pocket and make you pregnant.

From Olive view When we first came here to live I was asked by our neighbours to get a bag of horse food, so off we went to the animal food suppliers for a sack of horse food. The man could not understand me, so again I asked for a sack of food for a horse, a 40

kg sack. Still the man could not understand me, so off he went and came back with a sack that had pictures of animals on it, so I pointed to the horse, I had asked for a sack of food for an onion.

By Fyfin We were in our local supermarket, there was an English guy talking to the Spanish assistant, who spoke no English. A lot of gesticulating went on and the assistant went to another part of the shop and came back with a hammer. It was not what he wanted so he asked us "What is the word for fly".
When we explained to the assistant that he wanted a fly swatter "matamosca" there was laughter all round.
I said a hammer would probably have worked but his wife wouldn't have approved of the holes in the wall.

From Felicia I was asked to translate the sentence "the policeman rode into the crowd on his big white horse" into Spanish. Horse in Spanish is caballo and mackerel is caballa.
Guess what I said?

From Silvi I went to the store and asked for: burro sin sal. She gave me a strange look...i found out that i was asking for a donkey without salt (mixed up with Italian.... Burro ital means butter, Spanish would be mantequilla)

From Paul My partner asked for Queso entre piernas in a supermarket..... it should have been queso Entrepinares. The first is cheese between the legs

From Bob My wife and female host Cari were bathing in the sea. Suddenly I noticed that there was a bit of a commotion going on and I went to see what the problem was. Cari explained that my wife had insulted her. It transpired that Cari had made some comment about the brightness of the sun making her squint and my wife had helpfully taken off her sunglasses, offering them with the words "Put on!", "Put on!" I told Cari what my wife meant, and I explained to my wife that the Spanish word putona was an insult meaning 'slut'.

Mistakes I have seen in menus translated from Spanish to English, e.g. Rape a al marinera translated as "Rape in the sailors style", rape being Spanish for "monkfish".

From Andrew My friend was reading the paper one day and told her husband, 24 nuns were suffocated on a flight, the word for nuns is monjas. But it was 24 monkeys the Spanish word is mono.

From Bob During a group conversation about music I proudly announced that I had been to an outdoor concert to see Los Tres Tenedores. I couldn't understand why I brought the conversation to a complete stop, but the puzzled looks told me something was wrong., I said: 'You know, Pavarotti, Carreras and Domingo'. It was then explained to me that what I had seen was Los Tres Tenores, 'The Three Tenors' and not 'The Three Forks'!

I remember telling a group of Spaniards about my first visit to Spain when I was 18. I tried to go hitchhiking, but without much success. One of the factors in my lack of success was, I explained, the huge rucksack on my back. Unfortunately, I confused the word for a rucksack una mochila with the word for a beetroot una remolacha.

From Jake My friend's 7 year old son broke his leg in the Sierra Nevada at New Year. They needed an ambulance from Granada hospital to their home in Gibraltar. My mate spent all day on New Year's Eve walking around Granada trying to find an ambulance company. He eventually found himself almost begging a man in bad Spanish to help. The gentleman was very apologetic and kept holding my friends hand, and saying sorry and almost weeping because he couldn't help. My friend couldn't understand why the gentlemen was so upset , until he passed the shop again the day after and realised it was a funeral shop and the guy thought he had just lost his son. Can you imagine what type of vehicle would turn up to take them to Gibraltar?

RAMONAS SHOP

I have mentioned Ramona's shop before, in which I described how she was robbed several times each time putting a stronger door on the place until the thieves went through the wall instead because it was easier and how the hapless cops in this part of the country did not even turn up to inspect the robberies or take finger prints until the fourth time it happened. Anyway she deserves a paragraph because it's the only shop I know around here that stays open seven days a week, Christmas Day, New Year's Eve and just about all of the numerous holidays they have over here. Impressive enough if you have a team of helpers or large family to help, but she does it all on her own. Her husband, who is normally drunk and not good for much, never helps. He was the one who turned up at midnight at my home brandishing a shotgun in the pouring rain, I think he was after wild boar but could not be sure. I could see his outline through the glass door pane and it scared the crap out of me. The thought crossed my mind that she had told him that she had given me a cheap bottle of aftershave for Christmas. Drunk as normal, all he wanted was to ask me if he could leave his car in my drive whilst he went shooting defenceless animals. Anyway so far all this has been mentioned before, so back to her shop. It is all on its own in the campo with the word Comestibles written on its faded yellow frontage. You can get just about anything you would need in an emergency, even if you do pay slightly over the odds. On more than one occasion on staring at a half tin of peas and some stale bread, her little shop has come to my rescue.

The rickety bench and couple of old chairs under the tree on the other side of this country road has become the meeting place for several of the local men, who for one reason or another seem to have plenty of time to sit and drink cans of cheap beer. Their rota system allows for one or other to stagger across the road to buy another round of cans from Ramona. I suppose that they only buy one round at a time so that it's nice and freshly cold from her freezer cabinet. God! I hate cold fizzy cheap lager, it sure isn't beer. They are usually accompanied by one or two scruffy dogs who always go to sleep in the middle of the road. I could weave around them if these same men hadn't parked at extraordinary angles jutting out on both sides of this narrow road. It looks like they all skidded to a halt in desperation to start drinking. What with the dogs and the cars and a complete indifference of these guys to do anything other than stare at you, as if you shouldn't actually be driving past, it is like weaving around a half constructed barricade. They also seen to devour bags of crisps and squeeze fresh lemon on them, everyone to their own taste I suppose.

Just a few yards further on I nearly crashed the car whilst staring at a group of portly older women dancing some kind of fandango, with large shawls. I later learnt that it was an extension of the local keep fit group, not content with walking determinedly every day down the road, they had now taken to dancing down it as well.

It's no good going in there if you are in a rush, it is a place to meet the locals or at least stand politely at the back whilst several generally old ladies natter about friends and family for what seems like eternity. The worst time is when the locals who grow a variety of crops on their small holdings try to sell the produce to her, endless sacks of green beans, that all have to be weighed and measured so that Ramona can make a profit on re-sale. But it has a charm, like stepping back to a time when you did not have supermarket style delivery. Apart from food, she stocks just about everything you need in an emergency. Plasters. Socks, light bulbs, paint, pans etc. You name it she has probably got it stuck in a box somewhere.

I learnt from others that Ramona was something of a healer with her hands; she had apparently cleared up someone's shingles and was held in some esteem by the older locals. I did think about asking her to see if she could touch my shoulder and legs, which give me such pain. But it would only take her inebriated husband who also sits under the tree opposite, to come in and find me bare chested and possibly without my trousers, in innocent physical contact with his wife and I would be running, or at least limping down the road being pursued by a wild man with a shotgun.

MY CAVE TOILET

Part of my master plan has always been to separate up my rambling cave house into three parts. Some years ago (before I fell off the roof) I got it together enough to convert one end into a separate self-contained home, which friends now live in. The other end was going to be done in a similar manner, but has rumbled on for several years. The idea was that there would be somewhere clean and tidy for visitors to stay whilst I lived in a degree of squalor in the middle section with numerous dogs and cats. Finally it is now at last getting closer to completion with the building of a new bathroom. Having done over half of it things came to a standstill, for a long time, until my friend took over and completed the grovelling around plumbing type jobs, which my knees would never forgive me for. The problem is that the floor level inside is lower than outside, and as there is no sewage system except a potho-negro, it posed a bit of a problem as shower water and waste needed to go uphill. Now any intelligent person would simply buy a pump and masher, but not me. I put the loo on a plinth, so now you have to ascend to the throne. Likewise I had to raise the shower cubicle so now due to the low cave ceiling only people less than five foot six can use it comfortably. Yes I know, dumb arse that I am, but I'm only a paper pusher, what do I know about water levels. Anyway it all works, but guests seem rather reluctant to use the throne, it makes them feel a bit exposed, sitting up there in majesty, surveying all below them. The other problem was that the room was originally a walk through, so until I eventually blocked one end in, anyone who did not lock both doors, was likely to be surprised by passers bye.

MORE STRANGE FIESTAS

In the village of La Font de la Figuera near Valencia, the local folk celebrate the arrival of a new year, by stripping down to their underwear and running through the streets. One important point if you are going to join in next year, the underwear must be red.

Spain's version of April fool's Day, takes place on December 28th. In days gone by, children used to go from door to door asking for sweets, much like our Halloween. Bakers used to put salt in their cakes on this day to wind up the children. Apparently it's not allowed now, although torturing animals is. Most of this has now given way to more mundane activities like sticking paper cut-outs to people's backs.

In August Bilbao lets its hair down with a nine day festival, the strangest part being an ugly face competition. People who spend the rest of the year trying to make themselves as handsome, or beautiful as possible, attempt to transform their facial features into parodies of Worzel Gummidge. They then vie to pull the most revolting face possible. I believe the term is called gurning, toilet seat optional.

Not so nice

In the tiny Spanish village of Manganeses de la Polvorosa young men toss a live goat off the top of a 50-foot church belfry to the crowd below who catch the flying goat in a canvas sheet. This is derived from a tale where the priest discovered a goat in the tower, it became frightened and it leapt from the belfry. Surviving the great fall and landing on its hooves, the goat quickly recovered and disappeared into the woods. Nowadays the (not so lucky) chosen goat is hurled from the bell tower into the tarpaulins below, some survive the fall and some do not. If the goat survives it is revered and is paraded through the small village, becoming a local legend for years to come, otherwise they eat it.

Marking the end of Valencia's Feria de Julio, is the flower battle (*la batalla de flores*), established in 1892. Basically, falleras ride on parade floats, Young ladies defend themselves with tennis rackets and allow onlookers to pelt them with heavy little flowers then after everyone picks up the remains and pelts each other, no doubt including horse manure.

The filthy festival of Cascamorras takes place every 6th September when locals from the Andalusian village of Baza re-enact a medieval dispute with their neighbours from Guadix by covering their bodies in oil and grease and pelting "intruders" with black paint and eggs.

The morbid Festival of Saint Marta de Ribarteme in Galicia invites people who have had near death experiences during the past year to celebrate the patron saint of the resurrection by bringing a coffin with them.

Human tower constructions (Castles) originated in Tarragona and in Penedès , were derived from Valencian dances. To build these human towers, everyone is conscripted, the stronger bulkier ones at the bottom and the nimble, light ones at the top. Needless to say the ones at the very top need a good head for heights. Only the brave need apply.

Olive Groves

GENERAL RAMBLING

WRITING

(Sorry about the initial description, too much info, I know)

I have been down with a cold all week, so not at my best and my brain seems clouded in a heavy fog, so even the simplest tasks seem like wading through treacle. It's really claustrophobic when your nose is all blocked up and you have to walk around with your mouth open like a goldfish, just to breath. When you eat and have a mouthful of food you end up gasping for breath and spraying bread crumbs, or worse everywhere. Being slightly asthmatic anyway, I end up sleeping propped up in bed, waking up every hour or so to check that I am still alive. The mouth feels like the Sahara Desert having been gulping air in its desperation to keep the flow going. This is possibly the reason I have decided to stay up tonight and keep writing. Funny that but at the moment I typed that last sentence, I started to yawn. So much for the power of auto suggestion. People say "oh I wish I could write a book, I have always felt that there was one in me, but I don't know where to start". Well it is actually quite simple, you start with a sentence, and then another tends to naturally follow it. Take for instance this whole paragraph; it came from needing to blow my nose.

Anyway in answer to that comment I have added a section from another of my books in which I try to explain my methods of writing; you will find it near the end in the final ramblings in an attempt to pad out the pages.

You will find this chapter drifts around with no particular sense of reason or structure; after all I am half delirious and indulging in a bit of free writing. That is when you are supposed to let go and just write or in my case type whatever comes into your brain at the time. It does not matter what you say just let it all out. Forget about literature or what people may say, if it's any good or just rubbish. Even spelling, construction and punctuation are out of the window for the present. The idea is that nobody will see it, but as you are now reading it, well what the heck.

My nose just cleared for one of those blissful moments and it's like breathing for the very first time. It only lasted for a few seconds and is now back to being solidly blocked. But it has set me off on my next musings. Those little moments of bliss that stand out like beacons on a drab day. You know, like when you have been dying for a pee and you finally reach a suitable receptacle. The next moments are, if not orgasmic, at least come in a good second.

The time I found decent back bacon, after years of miserable Spanish bacon strips. I rushed home and made a proper toasted bacon sandwich with decent ketchup and proper butter, the first bites were exquisite. Hang on I'm starting to salivate here. Back in the dark days when I first came here and you had to wait for that food parcel with marmite, cheddar cheese and decent tea bags. The next day was spent overdoing it on large mugs of tea and sandwiches.

Living in a cave and working a lot on the computer you sometimes forget that it's daytime outside, when you emerge and plonk yourself down, eyes closed with the warm sun on your face and colours dancing around your inner eyelids, for a few minutes the world seems right.

 The moment you step into a warm comfortable shower and the water cascades over you and your body goes into a little tingling spasm for just a second or two (or is that just me?) These little moments of bliss are very important and often come when you are not expecting them.

Along with a lot of other men, I suffer with a rather embarrassing condition. It is not something we talk about much, but it can affect us on a daily basis, sometimes several times a day and often at the worst possible moments. It is called IFT and there are very few cures for it. Intermittent Falling Trousers are a product of having not been given the right genes to create a waistline that actually holds our trousers up. Belts are a curse, I am sure a man did not invent them. They just never do their job, well at least not for more than twenty minutes in any given hour. I am sick of hoisting my pants up in public. The more holes you make in them the tighter you adjust it, even when holding your stomach in, they will guarantee to let you down, normally when you are carrying something that you cannot drop. Suddenly you are walking slightly skew whiff, as it's the only way to keep your trousers from seriously descending in public. No wonder young men have recently adopted the descending trouser and show your Calvin Kline pants image, at least then it looks intentional. I have given up counting the number of cheap belts I have purchased off street vendors; they are no good anyway, as the metal buckle bar always bends under the strain of your expanding stomach. This leads to a very quick decent of your pantalones! "Get braces" they shout, Yer! Have you tried them? Some have cheap clasps that snap off as soon as you reach for anything, others attach to your belt, so that baggy trousers feel like they are bouncing up and down like hooped clown pants. Anyway I hate the feeling of being held down on each shoulder, it's like having double car seat belts. So far I have managed to avoid having a bad incident in public, except that time when walking one of the shelter dogs who decided to jump at me from behind, thus revealing my less that trendy Y fronts to a passing motorist.

Socks are almost as bad but at least they don't make an embarrassing spectacle in public, unless in your semi-conscious state, on rising from deep slumber, you slip on two completely different ones, then sit on public transport with your trousers rucked up at the knees showing white calves and tasteful or not, different colour socks. One tip, don't wear those Christmas socks with holly and Santa on them when it's July. Boy I must have indulged a bit too much the night before (no I didn't go to bed with them on).   You can only really buy two kinds of socks, ones that restrict your blood flow by having elastic tops, or ones that slowly ruckle around your ankles (My spell check says I can have truckle, suckle, rankle or buckle, but apparently not ruckle, anyway you know what I mean.) After two or three washes they even attempt to work their way under your heels. I once had a pair of white sports socks that slowly reduced in size from a 12 down to something even a kid of five would struggle to put on. Mind you they did say NIX on the side rather than NIKE.

Fashion has always passed me by, being an ungainly shape, my motto has always been if it fits wear it, if it almost fits wear it, if it fits and is cheap, definitely buy it. If it fits with the addition of a bit of string, wire, rubber band or even glue, buy it. Like a good meal you never know when the next one will come along. Why do all the trousers on the second hand market, seem to have come from men with giant waists and short legs, or skinny waists and gangly legs? On that subject, why do all the clothes at these markets smell of stale soap?

HOW COME

How did one of my shoes gets so far under the bed that I needed the broom handle to retrieve it? I sure didn't put it there last night?

Why does it take seconds to make a mess, but absolute ages to clear it up?

Where did the other sock get to? It's not jammed behind the drum in the washing machine.

How come it takes two chapters into a new book before I realise that I have already read it - is my memory getting that bad?

How come you can stand for ages without luck, trying to remember what it is you are meant to take with you, but a mile down the road you remember?

How come I need to watch a YouTube video to find out ten things I can do with vinegar?

Why don't Coke, Jaffa Cakes, Mars Bars, Wagon Wheels and Heinz Baked Beans taste the same as they used to?

How come I can drink five beers and not have to get up in the night, but one cup of coffee and I'm up a couple of times. And why do three beers make me unsteady, but half a bottle of whisky has no effect?

How come my dogs know it's a minute to eight in the morning, just prior to the alarm going off?

How come I don't remember saying yes to a situation, but still end up involved?

How come you never see pictures of 'Slimmer of the Year', three years after they won the award?

How come nobody really cares that the planet is warming up and the ozone layer failing, that is the problem for future generations. Just as long as you can get organic vegetables, for your healthy diet?

How come the hair under my armpits and other lower regions is black, but the hair on my head is dark brown, and my beard is grey?

How come my dogs won't let me near their bowls but then expect to share my meal?

Why is everything always my fault?

How come I always feel guilty?

How come I forget important things, but remember rubbish.

Being six foot tall, why is every table and work surface too low down, causing severe backache. Each generation is meant to be getting taller, but manufacturers still think everyone is less than Five foot six?

Why is my flat pack furniture so keen to return to being flat, rather than stay upright?

Where did all my real teeth go?

What happened to all those years, suddenly I am old?

DAYS

You get up in the morning and for some reason it's harder than normal to pull your socks on, over the next hour you manage to fumble a few things, even drop and break a cup or tip half your cornflakes outside the bowl. You just know it's going to be one of those days. I think certain days are set aside for certain events. You can have the "perhaps I should just keep my mouth shut day" or the "Why do I keep bumping into people I don't want to meet day" or even "Why all these bills on the same day, day." Then there are days set aside for specific incidents that aren't necessarily to do with you. Today was 'escape trolley day'. Those of you who frequent the local Mercadona supermarket in Baza may have noticed that the car park slopes away from the shop. This is obviously intended to keep what little rainwater we get in these parts, from flooding the premises. However, it has a particular effect on any random trolley that finds itself free of a restraining hand, or the chain linking it to all the rest. I pulled up and got out of my car to see a young child delightedly freewheeling down the car park in a trolley. Its parent was obliviously stacking bags in the back of their car twenty feet away. I am not as fast as I used to be, but managed to grab the basket before it could slam into the end wall or another car. Having saved their child and pushed him back, you would think they would have at least thanked me, but instead they started verbally laying into the child for being stupid. Needless to say it wasn't the child who was stupid. Twenty minutes later I came out with my hands full of shopping and stopped to watch a mature woman chasing her recalcitrant trolley. It was creating elegant circles as it headed in the same general direction as the previous one. The ladies handbag was going for the ride as well. She was not particularly nimble on her feet and not able to stop it before it thumped into a parked car. Discussing the incident with a stranger who had stopped to watch, he related that a couple of days ago a motorist had driven straight into the long line of trolleys that an assistant had been trying to push back towards the shop. So in future, as every week of the year out here is dedicated to some saint or other then I shall put down in my diary that this week is

'Saint off Your Trolley' week.

Having been somewhat immobilised recently I have had the dubious honour of being wheeled around Mercadona Supermarket in a wheel chair. They provide a clip on wheelie basket that turns corners ahead of you, it's actually quite fun. Unfortunately as it fills up, the weight imposes its own will on you, and you find yourself turning into isles that don't exist every time the wheels come slightly off the straight and narrow. Crashing into rows of wine bottles is not a good idea, when your kind carer is pushing eagerly, but talking to a friend at the same time. A common complaint amongst people with various difficulties is the habit of others to talk over them, or even ignore them completely. It's the old "Do they take sugar" syndrome. Even after a few minutes in a wheelchair I can sympathise. It's as if you don't exist to everyone else. People just don't see you and even walk right into you. A couple of times I felt like standing up, even on one leg and shouting, "Hey, can you see me now?" Unfortunately my clip on trolley would not let me, Doh!

HOW THE OTHER TWO THIRDS LIVE

I apologies to anyone living in Benidorm, or any similar resort, especially if they actually like living there. It's just not my cup of tea, and also to any hippies in Orquivar, but then they wouldn't buy the book anyway.

Many of us moved to Spain for very different reasons, but the vast majority of Brits only know the Country from annual holidays, for the most part, spent at one of the numerous resorts dotted along the coastlines. Venturing far inland, often being left to those with a more inquisitive nature. After living for a year or so in a mountain village not far from the Mediterranean, I decided as an experiment to live the life of a Brit on a package holiday at least for three or four days or for as long as I could envisage standing it. After all you can't be critical of anything without at least sampling it.

So I packed my black socks, open sandals and baggy shorts and headed for a well-known resort, that comprised of endless bars and restaurants fronting a very packed beach and surrounded by tall hotel apartment blocks. Booking into a fifth floor apartment, I sat listening to my neighbours conversation through plasterboard walls. It was a corner apartment and in the two adjoining streets below you could hear the thump of bass notes from two discos and it was only early afternoon. 12 hours later they paused for a while, until starting up again the next afternoon. This was not a good introduction, especially as I found cockroaches in the kitchen cupboard and this was five floors up in a new hotel.

Escaping to the beach with my towel, sun cream, enough money to rent a deck chair and buy an ice-cream, I found that I was sharing it with what appeared to be thousands of others. I carefully picked my way through reclining bodies in various shades, from pale pink to bright red and many peeling and in need of medical attention. Uttering apologies for nudging, tripping and at one point kicking sprawling limbs, I eventually found a small unoccupied patch, all be it a bit near the waterline. Anyway as long as I wasn't fast asleep when the tide came in, I would not drown. (Does the Med have a tide?) I gave up the idea of a deck chair and laid my rather small towel down. It wasn't till I attempted to turn on my face after ten minutes or so that I realised that I had been resting the back of my head of a pile of barely buried fag ends. At that point I decided to abandon the beach and would come back early the next morning, before it got crowded. I would buy a cheap child's plastic spade and investigate the patch I would occupy for any other surprises. Needless to say I did not return with or without the spade the next day because by then I had a hangover.

I decided the next thing to do was investigate one or two local bars. The first one presented me with the chance to play bingo with half a dozen bleach haired mature ladies and a couple of blokes in Scottish tartan patterned shorts, I later learnt over a beer that they came from Manchester and had never been anywhere near Scotland. To my surprise I actually won a small furry stuffed cat, which I gave to one of the ladies who said she never won anything. By the time I had played five games and drank three beers I was beginning to feel more relaxed. Looking for something to eat and true to my new temporary persona I went into the first bar that advertised British food, including a large fried breakfast at any time of the day. Not having had my ice cream or anything since an early morning tostada, I opted for the big fried breakfast; after all it was only teatime. That was a big mistake.

If it's one thing that really puts me off a fried breakfast, it is runny eggs. The pair of eyes staring up at me could have run off down the road if they wanted too. I called the waiter and asked him to take them back and flip them. When they returned they had assumed a greasy blackish colour with a griddled pattern on them, as if they had been run over by a leaking diesel truck. Still the rest of the meal looked ok so I pushed them to the side and concentrated on the rest. The bacon looked good so I cut a slice and put it in my mouth, now I may not have a subtle culinary palate, but I know mould when I taste it. Suddenly I lost my hunger, got up and left without paying; luckily the waiter did not see me go.

So far my experiment was not going too well, but undeterred I went souvenir shopping. It was a hard choice deciding if my mountain neighbour would like a plastic gnome sitting on the toilet with 'Welcome to Benidorm' painted on the bowl, or a photo in a floral frame of the skyline featuring numerous tall apartment blocks against an over vivid sunset. Who buys this type of crap? In the end I opted for a bar of Toblerone, everyone likes chocolate.

I needed to sit down and review my progress and make notes so that I would not forget when it came to writing this down, mind you that was not likely as it was searing itself into my memory quite well. The beach was out of the question and so was my noisy apartment, the cockroaches were safe for another few hours. Finally I found a small bench overlooking the sea and settled down to scribble my notes. Why is it that whenever you want to be left alone, somebody has other ideas? The guy was obviously a Brit; he had the same black socks, sandals and type of shorts that I was wearing. I took note that his open shirt revealed a gold medallion on a chain. I thought only ex gangsters who fled to Spain wore them. Maybe he was famous and wanted by the police across Europe. But no! Turns out he had just retired over here and was preparing to go and play indoor mat Bowls with other Ex Pats. For the next half hour I listened to his potted life story politely, there may have been something worth relating, but there wasn't. I did not let on about my experiment, but told him a lie about looking for a property to buy in the area. That was also a mistake because he then decided that he would be ideal for showing me around as he had just gone through the same process. But first it would be good if I went with him to meet his new friends and play a round or two of mat Bowls.

The small hall was in a nearby town and obviously a den of Brits. A small bar, two dart boards, some tables at which people in various states of decay were playing bridge and along one side a wide strip of fake plastic grass, obviously intended for Bowls. It was to this we headed after first procuring a beer, 'blimey bottled John Smiths!' I was introduced to several people and before I knew it tomorrow was all arranged for me, we would be scouring the area for my new home, but not too far out, so I could continue to attend the club and see my new friends. OK, so I am shallow, and they were genuinely friendly and welcoming but I could feel a dread creeping over my body. It only faded when after two games spent doubled up watching my balls slowly creep down the mat, I had serious back ache. Uttering apologies about being a newbie, I retreated to the dart board, where I could at least hold my own. After all, forty years earlier I had wasted three years at college playing it and table football, surely you don't lose the knack, and yes you do.

Somehow I was still there approaching midnight, maybe because medallion man had given me a lift and I had no idea how to get back to my apartment from there, besides which I had imbibed rather a lot of John Smiths. It didn't help that my new friend no longer seemed to be around. Apparently at some point he had departed on medical grounds, and left instructions for somebody else to take me home. This turned out to be a nice lady who insisted that once I was settled in the area, I should become one of her shared dining circle. Each person took it in turns to cook a meal for the group. I pointed out that my culinary skills were so bad, that I would probably poison everyone.

The next morning and with my headache, I was met in the foyer by medallion man, who had obviously recovered from his ailment, plus two other gentlemen. They had ridiculously dark tans, no doubt acquired lying on the beach, playing golf or lounging on a recliner beside their swimming pools. As I had almost consistently worn work trousers or jeans in my village, my now bare pink legs were in stark contrast. At that point I should have come clean and told them the truth, that I wasn't looking for a house and even wild horses could not drag me here again. But I was too feeble and just went along with it. We set off and George who liked to be called 'Rolly' for some reason and who was obviously an unregistered estate agent, led me around four hideous properties, whilst I pretended a degree of interest. Someone had painted the interior walls of the last place bright yellow as if the sun outside was not enough. We did have a rather splendid liquid lunch in a bar that looked run down from outside, but served some great tapas. The afternoon kind of drifted by after four beers at midday, but a further two properties including one that was well out of town and described as rural but actually overlooked rows of greenhouses, did not inspire me much. When I crashed out on my bed early evening, the beer and the sun made sure that even the thump of the disco did not keep me awake. Their parting comments after I had said I needed time to consider possibilities, was that they would call for me later, as there was a bar nearby where the barman spoke good English.

The thump on my hotel door woke me from a deep sleep, I think the dream was about becoming Benidorm's Mat Bowls Champ, but I can't be sure. They gave me time to splash some water on my face and say goodbye to the cockroaches and then we were off.

Karaoke has never been my preferred form of music. The Japanese, judging by their violent TV competitions have always been rather masochistic, so I suppose they are ideally suited to have invented it for bored business men. So arriving at a bar and finding a slightly drunk couple of girls singing "I will survive" completely out of tune was a cruel way to start the evening. The amazing thing was that the audience seemed to be enjoying it. Am I so really out of touch with modern society that this sort of noise is preferred? Maybe I am, after all I could never get my head around Rap, Rave or Hip Hop. They were right, the barman did speak English, but then again he had spent fifteen years driving for a brewery in the Midlands, so it was not exactly surprising. Now my Spanish is just about passable, to keep up the impression of a newbie I never let on, in fact I had somehow managed to acquire a nasal Luton accent from somewhere. At some point during the next three hours I imbibed rather too much alcohol and found myself giving a rendition of "He's not heavy he's my brother" and after what I thought was enthusiastic applause, but was most likely just polite clapping from my new friends, I launched into "Nights in white satin" which was in hindsight not a good idea as it starts off with fairly low notes, but soon reaches for upper registers and the need to clutch my gonads in an attempt to get there. After that I promptly sat down, much to my relief and most likely the audience as well.

This experiment was certainly upping my alcohol intake and when I hit the sack that night, it was a second bout of deep sleep uninterrupted by the thumping discos. I can see how many ex pats end up worse for the drink in these parts.

I had one day and night left so decided to stay out of the way of my new friends, find someplace to chill out or heat up, find a cosy bar and food that evening then head home the next morning.

"Hi, I called at the hotel, they said you had gone out with your beach towel early."

Oh no, I groaned inwardly as I opened my eyes as I lay on the sand. As my focus slowly adjusted I recognised the face of the lady who had given me a lift home, now staring down at me. The beach wasn't over crowded at that time in the morning but it must have taken her a concerted effort to find my reclining body. I wonder how many innocent males she accosted before she woke up the right one.

"Don't let me disturb you but we are having a Bridge afternoon and then a meal a bit later, thought it would be a good time for you to meet some of us."

Desperate for an excuse, I explained that I did not have the foggiest how to play bridge, and would only spoil it for the others.

"Oh! Well I am sure Geoffrey would be only too willing to start teaching you the basics, he loves imparting his knowledge."

"That's very kind of you but I really don't have the time, as I am looking at more properties later."

"Oh that's such a shame; still, you must come for dinner tonight at least."

I didn't feel I could refuse, so I agreed to come. Elsie handed me a piece of paper with very explicit directions and a neat handwritten map, then left me to my sunbathing.

Surprisingly I found the place fairly easy despite hundreds of identical block houses in rows; I can't believe they call them Villas. Her map was very accurate. After ringing the bell I was greeted by Elsie who had obviously gone to great lengths to hide her age with lashings of makeup. She wore a slightly revealing top, which really isn't a good idea when your boobs have sagged.

It was ominously quiet behind her, I had expected the hum of talking from a group of players arguing over who had what deck of cards. We entered the living room and several stern faces turned at the same moment, the only empty chair must have just been vacated by Elsie.

"Look you are obviously in the middle of a game, don't let me disturb you, I can go find a bar for an hour and come back when you have finished."

I could see from their faces that they thought this may be a very good idea; there was definitely a frosty look about their welcome. I made a mental note never to interrupt card players when they are in the fevered throws of competition. It was probably the same for Bowls, Monopoly or even Tiddlywinks.

Elsie was having none of it and suggested that I took a nice beer and relaxed in her sun chair beside the communal pool that was shared by ten apartments and situated out the back. I retreated whilst they all played on and it was actually rather nice, dozing in the late sun, with a cold beer.

All good things never last long enough and before I was ready to face the world again, five or six of the card players came out dragging an assortment of chairs and began to talk animatedly about the outcome of the games and why so and so had not played such and such at a certain moment. I'm the same when it comes about talking about dogs, so I don't begrudge them their particular interest, it was just that it had been blissfully quiet and now it wasn't. After pretending sleep for a minute or so more, I gave up when it was obvious that they were not going to respect my situation. Giving an amateur production yawn I sat up and smiled at the nearest couple, receiving a polite if unwelcoming nod in return. It was becoming obvious that a non-bridge aficionado, gate-crashing their select group was not appreciated. It upset the balance of their equilibrium. It was only Elsie who seemed unaware of the situation, as she breezed out and served everyone drinks, announcing that the meal would be ready in about forty minutes, but nibbles were on their way. 'Oh God' I thought I have got to try and hold conversation with them or leave, never to be seen again.

Luckily Elsie returned with food which filled up five minutes without having to say anything, then because she was one of those who is supremely organised in the kitchen, she propped herself next to me, and proceeded to force those nearest to include me in their conversation.

It was only a few minutes later that it dawned on me that her arm which was resting very close to mine and occasionally touching, was not totally accidental, likewise the flashing smile she kept giving had definite undertones.

'Oh my God', the woman fancies me.

When I was a teenager flirting seemed very natural, part of life's pleasures. The older I got the weirder it became, may be not for you, but certainly for me. Playing footsy under the dining table during the meal, with a sixty year old woman, who still thinks she is twenty, is definitely weird. I am sure all the others knew what was going on. Actually I wasn't playing footsy just trying to move my big feet out of the way, but hers kept following me. At one point I excused myself and went to the bathroom, but as I came out she was standing in the hallway, and we had to brush past each other, I had to move quick, any hesitation on my part, and she would have pounced, I believe they are called Cougars.

I really hope Elsie finds someone special, she was kind and helpful, but not for me. I have mentioned this before, but the men almost always pop their socks first and this has left numerous older ladies, particularly on the coast, on their own.

To my shame I told a few lies, beat a hasty retreat and made my way back to the hotel. As she bravely waved me goodbye, I could see that she was very disappointed, I felt a heel, but what can you do? The next morning I decided enough was enough and it was time to retreat to the hills.

How the other third live, part two

It was not my intention to continue my investigation into how other sections of the British communities in Spain live, but then I gave a lift to a 'crusty'. According to urban culture a 'crusty' is a young person who is homeless or travels constantly, has a shabby appearance and rejects conventional values. They have butt flaps,(don't ask) facial tattoos, lots of patches, dread locks, punk rock hair styles and often canine animal companions. Those in a relationship often have several miniature versions of themselves running around, usually with more hair than trousers.

He had been down on the coast, busking and trying to raise some money before returning to the commune near Orqiver. He invited me to stay for a meal and meet some of his friends. Dressed as I was in conventional cotton trousers and a Marks and Spencer's casual shirt I was a bit doubtful that I would be welcomed.

The hillside outside of the town was like nothing I had seen before. Admittedly in my younger days I had been one of those covered in mud at outside music festivals and living under a bit of tarpaulin for three of four days. But this had taken the basic concept and turned it into a city. Just like in any town there are those who can only afford basic accommodation and those that live in swanky homes. These old hippies were no different. One couple and three kids were squeezing themselves in to a two man tent with an extension covering attached to a nearby tree. Yards away someone had managed to build a geodesic dome complete with solar panels and I suspect an inside toilet. This was a luxury not afforded to the majority who lived there. You could see the well-worn path that must have led to the communal crap area. Personally I decided to keep what was in my bowels for as long as possible.

I have to admit that I was made welcome once it was explained that I wasn't somebody from the local council, or an undercover cop. Mind you even the police would have made a better fist of trying to blend in. After I had refused my third offer of a joint, I came up with the excuse that I was an asthmatic and it would be bad for me, they gave up trying to offer me any kind of drugs for free or for money, and settled for offering me a beer. Glancing at the bottom of the can which looked a little rusty I saw that it was only two years out of date.

The smoke from the bonfire around which we sat for what seemed like hours, doing relatively nothing, began to have an effect on me even without a few splifs. It was obviously not just old wood on it. And after the first hour I also began to lose track of time and started to understand how they could waste so much of it just grinning at each other. At some point my new friend got out his guitar and started playing. He was actually really good, and for his sake I hoped he had made a few bob on the coast busking. I remember years ago doing pastel sketches on the path near Brighton. Most just ignored you, but by the end of the day I had a whole pocket full of small change. Eventually a local policeman made me rub my artwork out and told me to move on as I was obstructing the flow. Ever since then I have given a coin or two, to anyone who shows the initiative to do something on the street, even if they aren't very good at it.

Anyway at some point a meal was prepared, I was hoping that someone had gone and shot a deer in the King's forest and we could all sit around watching it turn on the spit, like merry men and women. But I should have known that most of them were vegetarians. I have nothing against that; I was one for seven years after doing a holiday job in an abattoir when desperate for money. I still have a lot of opinions about mass animal production techniques, but I was born with teeth meant to eat meat, and I like it. I know it had rice in it; actually it was mostly rice with some green bits of vegetable if you were lucky. I still can't believe I fought desperately with my spoon in the communal bowl, to capture what looked like half a cauliflower stork. Three more rusty beers, a bit more campfire smoke and I was already considering to opt out and curl up in the corner, but not too near the communal loo.

There was a guy I got talking to who was about the same age as me. It turns out he had been an accountant for one of the big banks in London for thirty years. He had left behind a smart home, BMW and what had appeared on the surface to be a happy family environment. He had not told anyone, what he was going to do, one day he walked out of his front door and never returned. He made one phone call to the police to tell them that he had not died and there was no need to search for him, then caught a plane to Spain and had lived much like this for the last twenty years. I asked him if he was happy, after a long pause he said, no! But he never elaborated on his reply, so I changed the subject. Some people, in fact, on consideration, most of us never find what we are really looking for.

I slept that night on the ground near the fire and have to say it was temporarily liberating, until about four in the morning when I woke up shivering, and retreated to my car. The next morning I thanked everyone and wished them well, then drove home for a nice shower, with plenty of soap.

Garden Path

MORE HEALTH STORIES, part 2

I love the Spanish health system, not because it has done me many favours recently (although actually it has) but it gives me so much great stuff to write about and in general moan. So here is a Chapter about my latest escapades with doctors and the hospital.

A day at the hospital

My love hate relationship with the Spanish health system continues. Some of you that live near me may even visit the same Doctor in Benamaurel. No names but she has never once examined me in the ten years I have been here. I think if I told her my leg had fallen off she would still not get out of her chair and come around to take a look. I got the impression that she did not like me, because she was always abrupt, never smiled and send me packing each time as soon as possible. However my friend said that she did the same to him. One day he asked her if she was ok, and she actually admitted that she didn't like patients.

Anyway - The following observations were made in the waiting room of the local hospital after she passed me hurriedly on to them when I damaged my already damaged leg. As usual I get bored waiting, so start scribbling on bits of paper from my pockets including bus tickets, a paper tissue and the back of a business card some guy gave me when I tried to make enquiries about council tax last week, I call them observations but really I am just being nosy.

Anyway the reason I am here is that although coping on one and a half legs for almost two years since the last operation, from time to time even they pack up under protest and I'm left shuffling around like a stranded mammal out of water. I knew it was an omen when I saw the second hand Zimmer frame for sale in a junk shop. What is even more worrying is that I was on the point of buying it. If it's still there next time I pass, then I will definitely purchase it, it could be a good investment.

Well I'm sitting here in the Waiting Room and I knew it would not last, the smartphones have started appearing. I had a friend who was very proud that he had advanced from a mud hut to running an entire medieval city in some empire building computer game, it had taken him months. I asked him when he was going to fix his front gate, but he said he didn't have time at the moment, nuff said!

They have just called my name, so I rise quickly and head for the correct room, but apparently it was just to check that I was here and to have my own personal plastic wrist tag fitted. They would not let me put it on myself; do they think I am going to place it around another part of my anatomy, just for fun? Then they sent me back to wait some more.

I can normally get by with my garbled Spanish, but I learnt long ago when confronting any kind of authority to be well prepared. So I type out in advance what I want to say and use large black font, in case the medic has forgotten their glasses. Using Google translate gets you half way there, but it is apt to throw in the wrong word in inappropriate places. Thus it may say that you have 'a pain in the box' which could lead to some confusion, especially if you have attached your name tag down there. After they have read it, I try to elucidate further on my predicament, but by then they have normally decided that you need to be covered in plaster, put on a monitoring device or given an extremely painful injection in your rear end.

Great! Somebody who is obviously British has just started reading a book entitled "Grow your own drugs" actually I also have that book at home. It's more about herbs and spices than marijuana and the like. But it's a great title.

Blimey! An old lady has started knitting, are we going to be here that long? Maybe I should order a scarf ready for the winter.

I must have drifted off, there are now one or two new faces, hope my name wasn't called out.

"Donde John Moody"?

"Es hombre en el Rincon, Snoring."

A scan around those waiting reveals two possible broken feet, at least another two with back problems judging by the grimacing and constant stretching. Another couple seem to be sharing the same ailment; perhaps one is having sympathy pains. I remember my dog once developing a limp at the same time as me. When I recovered, his impediment went away as well. There is a mother and teenage son in the corner who seem to be sharing a private joke, which has gone on for at least ten minutes. They are both grinning permanently. To tell the truth it's a bit disconcerting in a hospital waiting room, it would have been alright at a comedy show. Meanwhile the old lady keeps on knitting, she seems quite content to spend the day here if needs be.

"You can see the doctor now."

"No thanks I want to finish these three rows first, damn! Look you have now made me drop a stich."

Why are a lot of hospital receptionists so officious? Being given a white coat just like the doctors, seems to give them an inflated opinion of their importance. I can understand that they spend all day coping with people who are generally complaining about something, so I suppose they just get hard. But they do get a wage and are supposed to be there to be helpful, so why are they nearly always indifferent, obstructive and in some cases actually what I would call rude. Or is it the effect I have on people, yep! That must be it?

The hospital had finally responded to my reclamation. I went to an appointment and they did an analysis and said the operation would happen in the next month or two. I said that I had waited so long that I was considering not having it done. They said that would not be a good idea as I could have serious problems in a year or so more. This is the third time I have gone through the system to the point of signing all the agreement forms then waited months with no operation date. When I returned home I was still unsure about having the operation, but then I slipped on a step and damaged the bad leg. Tests showed that I have torn some ligaments, one of the screws from the first operation is working loose and there is some displacement of the bone. Now I think that for my future health I must undergo this surgery. I hope it is well before or after my holiday. This hospital has let me down twice before now, so I am not sure when it will happen. The Medico said that it was not possible to say an exact date. I told him that it was not possible to tell him exactly how much longer I had to live, but he didn't understand my joke.

At last it's happened

In the last few years I have not been a stranger to the inside of hospitals. A hernia, false knee fitted, screws and plates fitted to a smashed lower leg and now a metal spike inserted up through my heal and into my leg bone, have all necessitated incarcerations of varying lengths. The latest saga saw me in and out three times in as many weeks due to post operation infections. Earlier visits gave me some good humorous ranting for my previous book, but I have to admit this time around there was little to rant about, they have been very good to me, pity it could have been a good Chapter. However, there are one or two things that are worth a mention.

The hospital room was dark, it was sometime during the interminable night. The street lights from Granada spread out from my third floor window cast enough illumination to be able to see details in the room. I was somewhere between being awake and half asleep when I shot bolt upright, somebody or thing was holding the toes of one of my feet. At the end of my bed was a figure draped in a white sheet, staring vacantly at me. It wasn't exactly night of the living dead at that moment, but it did set the old heart thumping for a second or two. My last two recent visits to hospital I had been fortunate to be given a single room, this time however I had to share it with an old guy who sadly was dying of cancer. During the day he was propped in a chair and said very little to his sister and son who turned up every day to sit with him but at night he turned into another person. Soon as the final lights were switched off he would start talking in a loud voice. Sometimes it was directed at me, but mostly I got the impression he was just talking to himself. Random bursts of sadness and humour punctuated by brief pauses would go on for what seemed like hours. As a result I got very little sleep for three nights in a row. I put up with it, more because of his condition and the realisation that one day that could be me. Talking back to him, and in the end telling him to shut up, had very little effect anyway. His other secret was that he could shuffle around unaided, as I found out when being woken up by him holding my foot. Up until then it took three nurses to lift him up and place him in a chair. His sister said he had not been able to walk for about a year, but that night he had climbed over the bed guard rails, come across the room and stood staring down at me. Then he turned around, shuffled to the main door clutching his descending oversized nappy, opened the door and disappeared into the corridor. Moments later lights all came on, sounds of rushing night staff and shouting for the next half hour of commotion as they strapped him back in bed and obviously gave him a knockout drug. The next morning his sister declared it a miracle that he could walk again. That day they sent me home, so I shall never know if it was.

I am never sure about the vast quantities of drugs we are instructed to take, I have a sneaking suspicion that the drug companies, re shape them, change the colours, repackage in different foil blisters and in boxes that appear large, but are mostly empty, and sell us them to us for a variety of 'cure alls'. I would not be surprised if the majority of them are just placebos, leaving our powerful minds to affect the changes we seek. During the last month I have been hooked up to a steady stream of liquid antibiotics, no kidding if you did a rough estimate, I must have absorbed over ten pints of the stuff, to cure a leg infection after surgery. It's a wonder we ever discovered the miracle of penicillin, if it takes that much of its offspring to affect a cure these days. The sheer amount I absorbed could have probably cured the Black Death in former times; do we take so much stuff these days that we have just become immune to medicine? At home I have two full drawers of out of date or unused pills. Not sure now which ones were for me, and which ones for the dogs. Don't think it would make much difference. I should throw them out, but for some reason still expect they could be useful, if it's a weekend and the pharmacy is closed, Ha!

Hospital questions

Do they think you press the red button for fun? The intercom crackles asking what you want. Do they want me to discuss if my problem is mild, serious or life threatening. No! It's just the man from the next bed is holding my toes.

Do the workmen just outside the hospital, realise its 3am in the morning and possibly not the best time to start drilling up the road. Ok! Maybe night rates are more lucrative.

The guy in the other bed, not content with talking all night has decided it's a good idea to leave his little radio on whilst he sleeps. A bit of soothing music would be ok, but when its tuned mid-way between stations and all you get it's a high pitched squeal or loud static, he's about to get a pillow thrown at him.

Some nights are so bad in hospital, interminable when you can't sleep. It's almost worth considering getting dressed, grabbing my crutches and sneaking out. Get a Taxi, find a good all night bar, and then sneak back in the morning. Not sure anyone would miss me; they would think I was in the toilet.

Why do they bring around a trolley at 11.30 at night, to ask if you want a drink, or a yogurt? Most people have a bottle of water by their bedside in case they are thirsty. So after they have settled everyone down and the lights are dimmed, they go and wake us all up again, daft!

Why don't they have a funny clown, jugglers, pole dancers, or comic entertainers touring around the wards to fill in the interminable hours? Sorry! Just being a bit sarcastic, Woman's Weekly (in Spanish) and a hundred puzzles for kids, is not exactly by type of reading matter.

More of your stories

I have confirmed this one is true, **from Peta**

I took the Duchess of Alba for a pee and tossed a bog roll over the top and hit her on the head, and then I bought her a plastic cup of lager and helped her back to her seat. I had no idea who she was till a week later when I saw her splashed all over the Spanish Hello magazine, and all 12 pages of photos of her inside !

From Beryl

I worked for an English Academy in Madrid and taught many business executives in some big businesses in the city. One of my students was a lovely lady who struggled to speak English, often using French words, so she made a pact with me that she would work hard the next weekend and would be able to tell me all about her weekend in English. The next week we met as usual and she sat down, took a breath and announced loudly, 'My husband is a very good cock"' I tried very hard to keep a straight face and managed to blurt out, 'Really?' 'Yes,' she replied proudly, 'he loves to be in the chicken!' As you can imagine, I could not contain myself and after I had spluttered out an explanation of what she had said, we spent the rest of the class howling with laughter every time we looked at each other!

From Susan

My husband and I went shopping in this department store. We went to the 3rd floor and bought a wine rack, after 39 minutes of shopping we went down stairs to pay and found everyone gone the shop was empty the till draws had been left open we tried to get out through the front door but it was locked, so I thought omg! Its siesta time they have all gone, my next thought was we are going to be locked in for 2 hours. It was so hot in the shop and I was dying for a pee, so my husband tried to open a back door and he must have set off a silent alarm as I looked out of the door 4 men came running to the shop and asked how we got in. We said we were locked in, they looked so embarrassed and gave us 20 % discount they we so nice if that had been Tesco we would have been searched and the police would of been called.

From Peter I went into a local shop, tripped over and took a complete shelf of items with me as I grabbed for support. Luckily there was no real damage, no glass broken and I was not charged for anything. The shop owner was very considerate, and said that these things happen from time to time, only last month a woman had dropped a bottle of perfume, it had stunk the shop out for days. I did not dare tell him that it had been my wife.

From Clive My car jack was broken and I needed to change a tyre by the roadside. Standing there for some time pondering possibilities, a van full of council workers pulled up. Eager to show off their strength they lifted the end of my car, and stuck a couple of blocks from the back of their van underneath, and one of them, seeing I was of retirement age, got down and changed my tyre for me. Then they lifted the car off the blocks, shook my hand and proceeded to go. At the last moment I asked them why they had not used a jack, to which they replied that theirs was broken as well.

From Bruce   The pet shop in my local town is quite impressive, with numerous isles full of items for different types of pet. I went in to buy a sack of dog food and left my dog in the car for five minutes. It was warm but not summer, so I opened the windows about a quarter. When I came out with my sack and opened the back hatch, I expected to see the happy face of my dog, but I soon realised he was not in the car. The passenger window had dropped into the door frame and he had obviously taken advantage. Looking up the road there was no sign of him, and I began to get worried because there was quite a bit of traffic. Suddenly there was a shout from inside the shop, and my pet came racing out, and even jumped back in through the car window. It turns out that the shop had several open sacks of food that people could buy by the scoop. Hidden from the counter Barney had sneaked in and was busily helping himself.

BEING CREATIVE

Einstein quote *"The beauty of creativity is it has no boundaries, no expired date and no exact rules or science theory of how it should be created. There is no right or wrong ,it will span wide like the universe and travel far beyond the unthinkable range of human mind, limitless and free."*

Well blow me down, is that what I have been doing?

The worst thing about being creative is that you are always setting yourself up for failure. Producing anything that others can comment on, opens your inner emotions up for criticism. I suppose many would say that by creating something and offering it up for appraisal, it is then your own fault if it receives negative criticism. This is of course true, but it still hurts when you have tried really hard at something and it gets panned or a luke warm response. Most people chicken out and never produce anything that can be examined by others. Mind you we can all feel the same emotions even in every day efforts. Have you ever cleaned the house before guests arrive, then felt uneasy as they wander around looking at everything. Even innocent comments take on a dark undertone. "Oh that's different," as they examine the wonky bowl you did at evening pottery classes fifteen years ago. If you catch someone surreptitiously or even blatantly running a finger along the window sill, it cuts to your marrow. Well just think how it feels when you spent hours, days, years working on something creative to be honoured with a "Hum nice, did you know my auntie used to paint, she did some lovely pictures." Now how is one meant to take that, "yes not bad, but I have seen better"?

I used to do craft fairs in the early days, putting my pictures on display most weekends quickly toughens you up to criticism. I remember two old ladies standing in front of my stall.

"That one's not bad, pity it's not in greens, not keen on autumn colours, do you think he could do it in green and a little bigger, it needs to go in that alcove under the stairs."

The other lady replied.

"Yes I am sure he would, anyway at these prices we should get one, it will be worth more when he is dead."

This was all done whilst I was standing there, but they gave no indication that I even existed, or could hear their conversation. The suggestion that I could pop my clogs was rather amusing as they were at that time a lot nearer the end than me.

Once in Covent Garden I had a man come up and ask me if I could knock out 300 of them by the weekend, as he had a new hotel and needed to fill it with original artwork. As it was already Thursday and I only had fifteen paintings I had to decline.

Someone else said that I wasn't a real artist, as I was trying to sell my work. He was not convinced even when I told him that Van Gough only painted sunflowers because he thought they would be commercial.

I suppose I am most sensitive about my art because it was the one thing I could do reasonably well from an early age and actually did survive from it for many years. The book writing is relatively recent since being in Spain, and I don't have any pre conceived ideas that it is any good, it's just something I like doing, even if nobody ever reads it, to be honest that's not quite true. Every creative person needs others to be aware of what they do, to some degree or other. My music making is another thing which helps fulfil me, but I definitely know my limitations in this genre.

There are basically three ways you can respond to criticism. The first is to have an ego so inflated, that you just can't see how you could be anything other than great. The second is to be exposed to so much of it over time that you become bloody minded and determined to prove doubters wrong, or the third is to have a lower opinion of your abilities than anyone else has. So when someone says "I like that" you mutter something about it not being one of your best. Actually there are probably more ways to cope with criticism, but I can't think of them at the moment. I suppose you could always punch them, only kidding.

Music

In 2016/17 (I typed 1916/17 but that would make me 168 years old) we lost many great musicians and entertainers. May be because I have grown up listening to them, that it feels more emotional than it would normally be when hearing of a famous person's demise. They formed the backdrop of my life, some more than others. A recent list of the top 100 most influential musicians and singers was composed entirely of people over the age of fifty and the majority above sixty.

I hope like me you grew up listening to music, we had it in our house from my earliest memories. Unfortunately at the time my parents, who were I would say religious, liked to listen to church music whenever it was on the radio and later the television. Added to that, my father's collection of records was 100% classical. We listened to Sunday half hour and I was obliged to sit through it. Later on I quite enjoyed belting out Jerusalem or, There is a green hill far away, but at that period in my life it was more or less torture. Likewise the whole two sides of Mahler's Pathetique, at the age of 10, was just plain unfair. Nowadays and especially after seeing 'Death in Venice' at least three times, I think it is a phenomenal bit of music.

At secondary school our music teacher had a hard time convincing any of us that understanding crochets and minims was going to be useful in life. (Everyone except Monty, my mate who had a natural affinity for playing, and was also far too brainy, and should have been next door at the Grammar School). But he came up trumps when he decided to form a group, must have been his idea as the rest of us could hardly play the spoons, let alone real instruments. I was trying to remember the name we called ourselves. I think it was Rugged Hum which was a nickname for bad smell. Anyway another mate found that he had a sense of rhythm so became the drummer and Tony, who had an idea how to strum a guitar, and I were also conscripted. I was given the job of bass player, as that was the simplest thing to do. Even then I never really got the hang of it. I was desperate to sing but for some reason they would not let me near our one microphone. I can't remember how I got it but rather than play a proper bass guitar, I ended up with a massive Ariston jumbo jazz guitar with pearl inlays and just used the bottom three strings. I really wish I had kept it, apparently it is worth a grand now, but back then I sold it for 12 quid.

We got good enough to play at a few local events and thought we were really cool by wearing sunglasses. Only trouble was it made it even harder to see what I was playing and I wasn't that good to start with. We split when time came to go our separate ways, but it started me on a path that still continues today.

Reaching the age of twenty after a few years being a suited, short haired bespectacled office boy in the council's town planning office, I left and went to college. Out went the suit and was replaced by flared jeans, long hair and marijuana. Apart from doing very little studying and quite a lot of drinking and consorting with the opposite sex, I also returned to playing music. We had a band of sorts that played what is referred to as Jug music, a type of early blues involving a mate of mine blowing into a stone jar to make a rude farting noise. If he got the rhythm right it sounded like a cross between a bass and a drum. He also had an assortment of harmonicas, a long plastic tube that if you whirled it around made a spacey kind of sound. His favourite instrument were a couple of old dinner spoons that combined with hitting his knee with them, they took the place of maracas. Olly was quite a showman and kept the audience amused. Just last year he came over to visit and resurrected his performance in a local bar, some of you may have even been there. John who was our main guitarist and singer was really talented. If you closed your eyes and listened, you would swear that he was black and at least a seventy year old blues man from the deep south of America. Our high point was to appear at college as the support group for an offshoot of Mungo Jerry; got a feeling they were called Terry and the Pterodactyls or something like that. They had a zob stick, comprised of a pole with hundreds of metal bottle tops nailed to it. Olly was well impressed and I think set out to make one.

Leaving College I started my teaching career, holed up in a one roomed cheap rented room, life became very different from the care free college days. My friends had all gone to different parts of the country. I had to start my social life again and finally wandered down to a local folk night. This eventually led to teaming up with some new musicians and we formed an electric folk band named Almontier. Again I was not allowed to sing except for a couple of funny songs. I guess nobody was brave enough to tell me that my singing was crap, sounded alright to me. We even sang on German radio for several weeks. It all fell apart when one of the guitarists committed suicide by gassing himself in his car.

My new job took me to a different town and so it was time to start all over again. This time I opened my own folk club, each week we had a guest singer or musician and the rest of the evening was for anyone brave enough to get up and have a go. During this period I was foolish enough to join an Irish show band. It was reasonable money as we played Friday night, Saturday lunchtime and Saturday evening, then again the same on Sundays, that's five gigs in a weekend. And this went on most weekends through the year in Irish clubs mostly in north London. Now three things made it difficult, firstly they were all Irish and drank like fishes. The accordion player couldn't play very well when he was sober, but once inebriated he was tremendous. Often when the band van was going around picking us all up he was missing and it would take an hour touring the local pubs to locate him. Once we just saw his arse sprawled over a privet hedge. They drank before during and after the gig and it was almost impossible to drag them away from whatever bar or club we were playing at. Sometimes it was just easier to head straight to the next gig. I had a beer or two but in general was mostly sober, so sometimes the hours waiting for them were interminable. That was the problem, they had all week to rest up, I had to be back in school teaching at 9 o clock on the Monday morning. I actually made as much with them as I did on my basic teachers' pay, and as I had a new mortgage every penny was needed, so I could not give it up. The second thing that was difficult, well actually very scary was that they would not let me drive the group van. The regular guy who was a kind of roadie was often as drunk as they were, but insisted it was his job. Hence the drive back which often took a couple of hours or half the night if they had drinking friends to visit on the way back was often almost suicidal. I just closed my eyes sat at the back and prayed. Once we pulled in at a fish and chip shop, but after a disagreement about how long it was taking to be served, the members of the band jumped the counter and took over the shop. We all spent the night in a police cell, and I never even got to have my chicken and chips. The last problem was that the Irish clubs we went to often had ties or at least sympathies with the IRA. I often saw leaflets being handed around and huddles of men earnestly discussing issues. Now imagine this, 500 Irish most of who are pissed, and one English guitarist. They had to announce at the start of the evening that I was English, but not to be touched as they needed me to keep my fingers. Hence I spent most of the night when not playing, sitting in the corner of the stage with my lonely pint. I could not even go and chat up a nice girl; she would be bound to have three extremely large building site type brothers in the audience. I lasted about six months before the Headmaster asked me if I was taking drugs because I looked so haggard and could not stop yawning. I admitted what I was doing and he issued me an ultimatum career or band, but not both. Within the year he gave me a promotion, so maybe he had a bit of sympathy for my monetary problems. One last point of note, the band was called the Johnny Cash Road Show, it was the manager's name, we always had big crowds, I wonder how many came expecting to see the great man himself.

The next thirty or so years past without much music on my part. Life and a career got in the way and I had other interests, my art was taking over and I had some success with it even winning an international award and exhibiting in Bond Street in London. There also followed exhibitions in several Countries. I was also into sport and despite breaking several bones over the years enjoyed judo, rugby and marathon running which buggered up my knees big time, but only after I had run five London marathons and trained up to a hundred miles a week, it was like a drug to me. Anyway we were talking about music. My guitars came and went but old faithful that I had since college followed me around gathering dust in various corners of rooms. Once in a while it would get picked up and strummed but nothing serious. And so it came to pass that I headed for Spain when I was in my mid-fifties. It got jammed in with all my worldly goods into my old Volvo estate and headed for the sun.

I suppose it was hearing all those great Flamenco guitarists, many who only made a living playing in the streets of the main towns like Granada and Seville that re awakened my interest. But there was no way on earth I was ever going to be able to play that sort of music, and certainly not at the blinding speed they could do it. It's a bit like Blues; unless you were born to it then it would always be a pale imitation. However, I tried and after hours and hours of my new found freedom, I managed to compose one piece of music that sounds half folk and half classical, but with a Spanish flavour. It's called Los Guajares, after the village that I lived in, and I still play it to myself from time to time, but never in public.

It's surprising just how many musicians there are when you start poking around the caves of Andalucía. Maybe it was the advent of pop music in the 50's that started generations of people brought up on a continuous outpouring of new (not often good) but at least inventive music. We all tried during the 60's 70's, to emulate or badly copy our heroes. The 60's was more my time, but 70's Stairway to Heaven, Sultans of Swing, Hotel California were good. Bit dubious about the 80's not so sure songs like The Final Countdown and Sweet Child of Mine is quite my kind of music. The experimental 90'and later Red Hot Chilli Peppers and Primal Scream had their place, I suppose. In my youth, all across the Country, spotty teenagers would form groups and most never got beyond playing at the local village hall. Folk clubs, jazz, blues, alternative, rock, you name it and there were clubs in most towns of some description. Anyway it has left us with many talented ageing exponents after a life time of practice, still strumming 'Smoke on the Water' or 20 verse Dylan numbers. Even out here in the Spanish hinterland, there are a few places to gather and jam with other likeminded souls, or you can take over a bar for the night and send out the message. We have had some great evenings, where people of all standards have been welcomed. There have even been a few karaoke events, not exactly my taste, but at least it gives those who can't strum, pluck or bang an instrument the chance to air their vocal chords and dream they are Elvis, all three Bee Gees or Sinatra. Although if I hear 'It's Raining Men', or 'My Way' just one more time, I may have to run out the door screaming.

My attempt at being an entrepreneur, by running a music festival was covered in the first book. You know when you start something and it then gets a life of its own and becomes a car without a handbrake on a steep hill. You hang on to the door handle in a vain attempt to prevent it running away with you. Well! Woodrot was just like that although more masochistically enjoyable. The nearer May got, the more I got stressed, what had started as a musical picnic was becoming a major local event. Trying to keep everyone happy, proved too much and with a lot of relief, but also a bit of sadness I gave it up. The council and friends in a local group have taken it over and it is now held in a marquee in the local village and under a different name. I can't say it has the same ambience as on my land, and although the Brits supported it in the afternoon session, it was disappointing that the local Spanish did not turn up in any numbers to listen to some good Spanish bands in the evening. I suspect they thought it was solely for the ex-pats, it needs some serious publicity if it wants to survive as an event.(It did not take place this year, so seems like the end.)

My efforts with the marching band and playing a saxophone were also detailed in the previous book, so won't go over them again. If you haven't read it - it's called 'Grumpy in Spain', and can be ordered through Amazon or direct from me.

In the past few years I have tried my hand at recording and producing my own CDs of my compositions. They are not bad, but the production quality is not up to professional standard. I have also collaborated with a Spanish friend on several CD's worth of self-penned songs from both of us. My latest project is to record a blues CD, depressingly entitled "Dead Men Walking", with another friend John. We may even form a group and perform locally, that is for the future.

Actually coming back to this chapter things have moved on. We now have a full band and have done several gigs, even being paid to do it, wow! Even resurrected Woodrot once more.

Young donkies

DOGS

One of my friends always starts yawning when I begin talking dogs with his wife, we can go on for ages. He says we should start a local radio programme called "Gill and John talk dogs"

The Rottweiler was abandoned and tied to the door of the dog shelter. Getting there early to open up, I approached carefully, there was no way past him. As I got within reach of his chain he started growling which to be honest wasn't the sign I was hoping for then he lunged towards me. Being brave, well actually having assessed exactly how far he could lung before being brought to an abrupt halt by the chain, I started talking to him in a voice you would use on a very young child. This did not seem to have much of an effect, other than to antagonise him further. He tried to lunge again and it was at that moment I realised that although the chain was fairly sturdy, it was actually attached to the door handle by a bit of string. As the blood drained from my face, I backed away and sort refuge in my car. When help arrived they didn't care much for putting their life on the line, so we all retreated to the local bar to consider our next course of action. Eventually we got hold of the local professional dog catcher who with the help of a long pole and loop, managed to get the dog into one of our portable cages. The idea was that he would take it away to the local council pound where its fate would be sealed. However it was his bocadillo time, so they dragged the cage into our premises and left him with us, never to return. It soon became obvious that this dog was almost blind and suffering with other problems. It must have been scared stiff, not knowing where it was and what was happening. We left it to calm down, gave it food and water and named him Rocky. It is fantastic when you see a dog change character once it knows kindness. Rocky the Rottweiler became a favourite with many of us, and was a happy soul, who was from then on so glad to hear our voices in the morning when we arrived. He loved going for a walk even if he did keep bumping into every bush and obstacle. His illness meant that his eyes were always infected despite a lot of medical treatment kindly paid for by donations and he also had a bad skin condition. Nobody was going to adopt him, the future did not look good, there was little more we could do for him. Then a kind lady paid for him to go to a good centre and he was treated by the vets at the medical college in Madrid. He improved a lot and we were sent videos of him happily eating with other dogs and cats.

Unfortunately it was found that Rocky had cancer and within a couple of months it was so bad that he had to be put to sleep. But at the end of his life he knew kindness with a lady who fostered him; I have a photo of them asleep together on a sofa. I deal a lot with abandoned dogs, but sometimes one comes along that affects you more than others. I suppose because the first time we met he tried to take my head off, but later would happily wiggle against my legs, made him something special.

GRUMPY IN SPAIN AWARDS

AWARD FOR PERSISTANCE

A year ago I saw a very fat old lady trying to peddle along a cycle path on a flat road in Baza. She was hardly moving, and judging by her wheezing efforts and pain filled face, was really struggling. A month or so later I saw her again, she was now moving at a slow but steady pace, and looked more comfortable. Last week I saw her; she had lost a lot of weight and was going along at a more rapid pace. Well done madam, you may never read my book, but you deserve a lot of praise.

AWARD FOR QUALITY

To Paco and Anna that run a local bar. The best coffee I have ever drank in a Spanish bar and the meat served in their restaurant is the best I have tasted. Don't know what they put on it but it's yummy, and the entrecote steak fills the whole plate.

AWARD FOR LACK OF IMAGINATION.

On the other hand most, but not all bars in this neck of the woods, think cuisine means a thin slab of lomo, a pile of pre-cooked chips and a runny fried egg, which hardly saw any heat.

AWARD FOR LACK OF CUSTOMER CARE

The countless shops were the assistants and customers prefer to chat than sell or buy. Whilst I wait patiently with a pair of new underpants waiting to ask the question 'Are they algodon or not?" (Cotton)

AWARD FOR AT LEAST TRYING

To Emilio and his bar, for attempting to reproduce the full English breakfast. It is a valiant effort, and deserves recognition, even if the toast isn't toast and the request to remove the runny yoke, by flipping, ends in disaster. To be fair they do it all on a flat grill, so there is no runny cooking oil to drizzle over the uncooked parts.

AWARD FOR BAD DRIVING

Don't have enough of these to hand around, to all the drivers who turn without signalling, and can't be bothered signalling at all at roundabouts, park blocking half the road, tail gate you, overtake on a corner then turn off seconds later.

AWARD FOR CONSISTENCY

This goes to my bank account which consistently tells me I am in the red.

AWARD FOR OPTIMISM

The small metal bridge is wide enough for a car, but you have to be careful because wider vehicles have forced the metal railings till they all vanished into the river, leaving sharp metal stumps that have claimed more than a few car tyres. Last week I saw a large lorry attempting to cross. Admittedly its tyres were fairly impressive in size, but it had to ride along on the shards on either side. It made it and drove off, hopefully without any slow punctures.

AWARD FOR COMPLETE STUPIDITY

This goes to me for falling off a roof five years ago and giving myself constant pain, problems and frustration ever since.

AWARD FOR NON PAIN RELIEF

To the local hospitals that insist that paracetamol is all you need for pain relief.

AWARD FOR MAKING THINGS COMPLICATED FOR NO REASON

Local councils, lawyers and just about any petty official are going to have to share this award.

GENERAL INFORMATION FOR ANYONE VISITING SPAIN

Particularly my area of Andalucía, but also other major cities.

Easter Week

Easter in Andalucía is a heady mix of faith, pageantry and raw emotion. It is the most deep rooted and heartfelt celebration of the year right across Spain. Centuries of tradition encompass the passion involved with the death and resurrection of Jesus Christ. This fervour plays out in all the major cities, such as Seville, Malaga, Granada, Cordoba and Huelva, and also numerous smaller towns and villages. Millions gather to cram the streets in order to see the magical and very moving processions.

Seville

Semana Santa processions include enormous 'pasos' (floats) which are carried through the streets by well-trained teams of 'costaleros' (bearers), and followed by hundreds of 'nazarenos' (penitents). The moods of individual processions change throughout the week. The most sombre ones are Good Friday, depicting the crucifixion, but on Easter Sunday they are much more joyful, celebrating the resurrection. The floats are incredible works of religious art, often dating back three centuries and depicting parts of the Easter story. The streets will be packed three or four deep along the route of the processions, which can take many hours to complete. In Seville, over 50 brotherhoods (cofradías) have two floats each, so that means a hundred separate floats trying to navigate the route. The Costaleros who carry the floats often only get one chance in a lifetime, because the demand to participate is far in excess of numbers needed. Basically it is male dominated, mainly because many of these floats weigh over 2,000Kg. The Good Friday processions leave their churches at the stroke of midnight and are carried all night, with enormous crowds following behind them.

Malaga

In Malaga, brotherhoods undertake religious study and then get involved in acts of charity in the community. At Easter they parade from different houses of the cofradias, and wander all over Malaga. Their headquarters are recognisable because they have giant double storey wooden doors, enabling them to get the religious icon floats out. Finally all the various Confradias converge on the Plaza de la Constitucion and the Malaga Cathedral. One common element is that many wear hoods and robes, making them look mysterious. The intention is that everyone is on the same level, not individuals, but part of a collective. That way only God would know who is who.

Granada

In Granada thirty two different Confradias wind their way down through the Albayzin and Sacramonte hills, the old gypsy quarter, located on the slopes opposite the Alhambra Palace. On Holy Wednesday, it is the procession of the Christo de los Gitanos, where large bonfires are lit on the hillside. Holy Thursday the processions become Christo de Silencio, the only sound being a beating of a drum to keep time. Good Friday is the Soledad de San Jeronimo, people dress up as historical figures from the Bible. Easter Sunday is the turn of the children carrying ceramic lanterns, which jingle as they walk. The Alhambra in Granada has always been a major attraction. The amazing tiles in the Nazarene Palace, the view of the city from the fort and its beautiful gardens are impressive. The summer months do get very packed and it is definitely better to go out of season, to fully appreciate it. It is also better to book in advance.

Other smaller towns such as Ronda which has fourteen processions, mostly crossing their famous and impressive arch, and Vejer and Arcos, where the carriers need special training to circumnavigate the tight narrow lanes and corners, also celebrate as best as circumstances allow. The "El Abuelo" procession that sets out in the early hours of Good Friday from the Cathedral of Jaen, is extremely moving and atmospheric.

If you only get the chance once to be present at one of these centres during Easter week, you will remember it for a long time, it is like nothing else you will have witnessed in a parade. The very air crackles with emotion.

MY AREA

Andalucía in August, where to head to avoid the crowds

It's as if a bell goes off at the beginning of August. Half the population of Spain, jump in their cars and head for the coast. Beaches tend to fill up, and main roads soon clog up. To my mind that would be the best time to head in the other direction and go inland, after staying at home for a few days just to let the mad rush subside. Andalucía has numerous hidden gems worth seeking, notwithstanding it is a verdant part of Spain, despite limited rainfall. Books have described it as the Garden of Eden. So where to go? Here are some suggestions.

Firstly you definitely need a car to explore this part of Spain. Driving around off the main roads will lead you to small villages, olive groves, Moorish ruins and panoramic views. It is known for its white washed villages, such as the beautiful scenic route through the Alpujarras and villages such as Pampaneira, and Bubion. Vistas are often set amongst impressive blue hazy mountain ranges, where olive green trees predominate. The villages stand out from a distance, shimmering in the hot Spanish sun. They appear timeless and in fact many of them have changed little over the years. They may have one or two roads that you can drive a car down, but off to each side are usually wonderful mazes, little alleyways that interweave between each other. You can lose yourself in the charm of it all; the busy world seems a long way away.

There have now been numerous popular books written by authors who have sought a quiet existence in such villages. Gerald Brennan, (South from Granada) and more recently Chris Stewart (Driving over Lemons) have described their own idyllic experiences amongst these Andalucian villages, where daily life definitely slows down.

Visit Ronda, one of the most interesting and historical town of Andalucía, and its impressive arch over a sheer drop. Ernest Hemingway the author referred to it as the most ideal town in the whole of Spain. The road from Algodonales near Cadiz down to Ronda (A374) is considered amongst the most beautiful drives in Southern Spain. You will see mountains, river valleys and lakes, springtime wild flowers and orange and lemon groves. If you can get a train from the coast, that is another stunning way to approach it. There is more to Ronda than its bridge; the town has two others, one Roman and the other is Arabic. Alameda Park has a lookout platform to take photographs of the panoramic countryside in all directions. Ronda has definitely one of the oldest bullrings in Spain that can hold over 5000 spectators. In September there is a Goyescas to celebrate; everyone dresses up in period costumes from the painter Goya's lifetime.

Also visit the National Parks such as Donana and the Sierra Nevada.

Cave houses, particularly around Guadix, take you back to a past time when people used to literally dig out their own home, in any available hillside. Little white chimney pots dotted around reveal that beneath your feet people used to, and still do, live in their hobbit style homes.

If you want to get your adrenalin pumping, visit the Caminito Del Rey, near Malaga, It is a newly reconstructed walkway clinging to the side of a cliff face above a stunningly beautiful gorge. Nerja on the coast has an atmospheric cave system, with an enormous stalactite; they even hold concerts down in its caverns.

Over 3,000 fiestas are celebrated every year in Andalucía; there is music, dance, excessive eating, exhibitions, fairs, carnivals and atmospheric religious processions. Almost every town and village has its own patron saint and feria.

April is the real start of the Feria season, try dancing Sevillanas and drinking sherry in Seville, or go on a pilgrimage, well at least a beautiful hike from Andujar to the National Park. Watch the world's longest horserace of 500km across three provinces, don't worry if you are an animal lover, they are very well treated.

Cordoba in May is time for a month of floral displays: crosses, the Patios festival and Ferias. In Jerez they also celebrate the Horse, with equestrian events and displays.

See Granada's Music and Dance Festival in the Alhambra, and stay up all night for the Noche de San Juan and see bonfires on the beach and people partying till dawn.

I obviously have an attachment to the part of Spain I live in, but it is such a wonderful large country of diverse landscapes and people. My favourite city is definitely Barcelona.

Barcelona

Barcelona is an amazing city to visit if you are staying anywhere in the Province of Cataluña. Most people visit the La Sagrada Familiar, Gaudi's incredible masterpiece of a cathedral, or the Ramblas with its 1.5 Klm of human statue performers, pavement cafes and great architecture. But there is also Park Guell, inspired by Gaudi, and the Barrio Gotico, the labyrinth old gothic quarter that is excellent when lit up in the evening, and a great place to go and eat. There are so many things to see that you need to stay a few days and if possible with somebody who knows their way around. There are places that people often don't realise are there, these often get missed, but are well worth visiting.

Below the streets of Barcelona lies its ancient past. You can walk the subterranean roman ruins; it is amusing to see the feet of today's residents passing the small windows set high in the walls. You are amongst the subterranean ruins, ancient stone chambers, streets and squares underneath Barcelona's Musea d'História de la

Ciutat (City History Museum) they include a factory where fish was salted and a wine-making shop where grapes were pressed and wine fermented in open vats. There is a Roman bathhouse, as well as pits for dyeing and laundering.

Pueblo Española

On the outskirts of Barcelona they have constructed whole streets representing different styles and areas in Spain. You are walking down a street in Galicia, and then turning a corner you are in Andalucía or La Mancha.

A UNESCO listed Art Nouveau Opera house incorporates grand staircases and columns and incredible colour and design; it takes you back to a lost era. This is the place to experience stunning opera or flamenco concerts.

Take the tourist bus ride that goes around the city stopping at many major attractions, start early, you can get off and on to give yourself time to visit these and many other gems in this fantastic city.

Santiago de Campostela

There is so much to tell about the majestic city of Santiago de Campostela. It is a walkable city in which you can lose yourself in the many stone paved streets of the old part of town. The place seems full of students, Pilgrims and tourists.

You cannot describe this city without first mentioning the Cathedral and its square the Praza do Obrodoiro. It dominates because no other building has ever been given permission to be higher than its towers. It is nationally famous for being the destination for one of the world's great pilgrimage routes, known as the Camino de Santiago, although there is more than one of them, depending on where you start from. Pilgrims have been travelling these routes for centuries as the remains of James the Apostle are meant to be stored in the Cathedral. The pilgrimage has become very popular in recent years and it is estimated that the church authorities have now handed out more than 198,000 certificates to those that have walked at least 100 Kilometres or two hundred if they used a bicycle. There is a festival of St James that takes place on 25th July, if it falls on a Sunday; it is regarded as a holy year; the last time this happened in 2010 approximately 12 million people visited the City that year. The Botafumeiro, which is a giant incense spreader and the largest in the world, can sometimes be seen swaying back and forth on chains and takes eight men to swing it.

Other great features of this place include the modern 'City of Culture' that looks like a giant scallop on the skyline. It houses a museum, library, and changing exhibitions. There is also the Museum of the Galician People, which is housed in in an old Dominican Friary. It has a tremendous spiral staircase and there is access to the beautiful nearby church and gardens. In contrast to the traditional, is the Galician Museum of Contemporary Art, situated nearby in the Puerta Del Camino? Both these last two museums are right next to the serene Bonaval Park which is nice and secluded, a perfect place to sit and contemplate life.

There are plenty of places to eat, but the locals and young students head for Rua do Franco near Obradoiro Square and Raina. If you visit this city bring your Pilgrim passport, student card or pension card to get serious reductions on many attractions.

Like any of the main tourist spots in Spain, don't expect to just arrive and find good accommodation. Always book in advance, especially well in advance if you are visiting for a festival. The town will be heaving with people.

If you only attend a Spanish fiesta once in your life, do it. You will be repaid with an experience that will remain in your memory.

THE COAST OF SPAIN

Another thing that Spain has to offer is its fantastic beaches. They encompass everything from tourist spots catering to your every need, right down to windswept open vistas and the tang of the sea.

The western Costa de la Luz is quieter than the tourist beaches of the other Spanish coastlines, but its beaches are wider, wilder and with less development. Rocky coves invite exploration, the landscape is more diverse, plus the towns are steeped in history. The Atlantic rollers entice surfers from all over the world, and Tarifa is the windsurfing capital of Europe. This part of the Andalucía's coast is home to both whales and dolphins. Known formally as **cetaceans,** some of them are up to 120 feet long and weighing 190 tons, heavier than a Boeing B-747. They can be viewed by taking specialist boat trips, particularly from Gibraltar or Tarifa.

Following the coast around

Cadiz is an ancient port which boasts a castle, an incredible cathedral, a long promenade and plenty of enticing cafés dotted around its leafy squares. Find a bar or club where genuine intense flamenco music is being played; you will not forget the experience in a hurry. Nearby is Puerto Santa Maria, from where Columbus set sail.

Moving on to the southern coastline, Malaga and nearby hotspots of the Costa del Sol such as Fuengirola, Torremolinos or Benalmádena, all provide for a more standard type of tourist holiday. Those wanting to explore away from the tourist towns, should head east towards the relatively undiscovered Axarquía. Towns in this region, known as *pueblos blancos* (white villages) are more traditional. Nerja is an interesting place it has an amazing cave system that is open to the public. It boasts one of the biggest stalactites in the world. The town is also very popular with the British who love the shopping experience.

Chris Stewart (Driving over lemons) and Gerald Brennan (South from Granada) made La Alpujarra popular, and the scenic routes around the sierras are stunning to drive around. Further to the west is Ronda and its famous bridge and drop to the chasm below.

Just in case this is all to slow paced for you, what about mountain biking along dusty trails and through remote Andalucían villages, or rafting on the Genil near Malaga. The resort of Chclana covers several sports such as windsurfing, horse-riding, diving and sailing. Then Andalucía gets really daring with the Tyrolean traverse ropeway at El Torcal. But the new big daddy is the recently opened Caminito Del Rey in Malaga province. Thee kilometres of walkway clinging to the rock face of the Garganta Del Chorro, it also has glass floor sections to really freak you out.

Frigiliana, a *pueblo blanco* with breath-taking views of the Sierra Almijara and Salobreña, home to a 10th-century Arab castle overlooking the sea, are definite places to visit.

Going east, there are plenty of characterful towns along the coast. Visit the picturesque Cabo de Gata and the Desierto de Tabernas , the only recognised desert in western Europe and background of dozens of Hollywood classics such as *Lawrence of Arabia, The Good, The Bad and The Ugly or Indiana Jones and the Last Crusade.*

Next comes the province of Murcia, visit the quaint village of Águilas, with its restored medieval Castle of San Juan and windmill museums, and notable Cartagena, one of the most historic Spanish ports due to its strong Phoenician, Roman and Moorish heritage.

Northwards from here lies the famous *Levante Español*, more than 500 km of coastline, host to some of the most packed resorts such as Benidorm, and Torrevieja. The city of Valencia is definitely worth a stop: tradition and modernism blend in Spain's fourth biggest city.

The nearby town of Sagunto, with strong links to Spanish mythical warrior El Cid and a stunning beach, is also worth a visit.

Now we are heading further up the eastern coast of Spain. The Costa Dorada (Golden Coast) starts in the province of Tarragona. The beaches here are usually packed, but inland areas are often ignored, in particular the gorgeous National Parks of Sierra del Montsant and Poblet. Anyone with an interest in natural landscapes would also do well to check out the Ebro Delta, one of the largest wetland areas in Europe.

Don't miss the Costa Brava, beyond Barcelona and along the coast of the Gerona Province. The name of the area translates as 'wild coast' but this refers to the rugged landscapes of some of its Riviera, not the gentle waters that bathe the coastline. In fact, the region holds a record number of European Blue Flags for its pristine, placid beaches, mainly around the villages of Calella, Lanfranc and particularly Tamariu. The town of Figueres, birthplace of surrealist genius Salvador Dalí (whose house-museum can be visited) and the surrounding coastal towns are less than an hour away on the motorway.

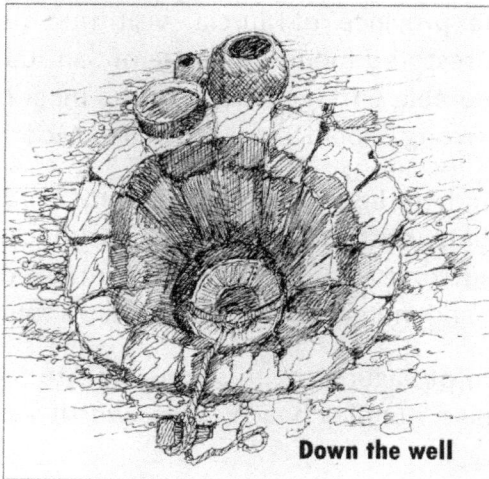

Down the well

I SWEAR IT LOOKS LIKE

Part of the problem of having a vivid imagination and being an artist is that you look at everything and often see something completely different in it, faces in tree stumps being the most common. I was driving along the road that skirts our local mountain Jabalcon, when I glanced sideways at its outline. I don't know if it was the low sun but I swear that I could see an Egyptian gentleman complete with fez, laying down and displaying a prominent erection. There was a tractor in front of me and an impatient white van behind, so I could not stop to examine further. Glancing again a few hundred yards further on there was no sign of the gentleman. I forgot it for several days and had not taken enough notice of the exact point, so when I came to look for it again I could not satisfy myself that the couple of rough approximations I came across were the initial image I had seen, they were not so convincing. I was so intent scanning backwards and forwards at a crawl, that I almost came off the road a couple of times, even cyclists were passing me. It's a pity because I was going to take a photo then elaborate on the outline with my drawing skills, and put it in this book. I have taken a shot that almost replicates what I first glimpsed, plus a couple of others that resemble a young girl and some kind of dead alien. I have seen some great cloud formations that look like faces and objects, the best one being a one fingered salute .Unfortunately I didn't have my camera with me, and don't own a smartphone. So the next couple of pages explain why I drive so badly when in this area, I'm busy looking for more images.

LOOK AT MY LOCAL MOUNTAIN,ANYTHING STRKE YOU?

TAKE A CLOSER LOOK,NOTICE THE SHADOWS AND OUTLINE OF
THE TOP OF THE MOUNTAIN

SURE LOOKS LIKE A YOUNG GIRL
WITH HER HAIR SPREAD OUT AND LAYING DOWN

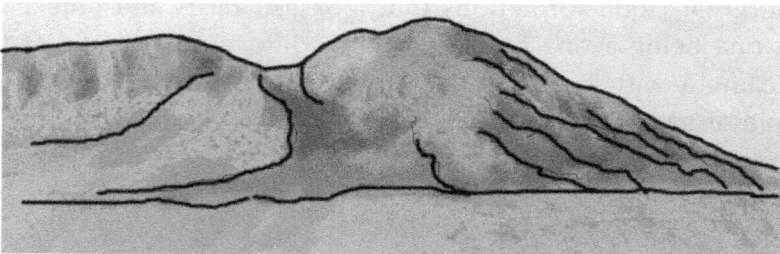

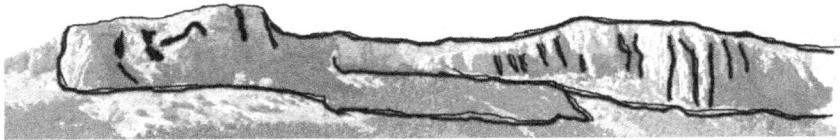

LOOKS LIKE A DEAD ALIEN OR MONKET TO ME

OK,THIS LAST ONE NEEDS A BIT OF IMAGINATION,BUT IT STRUCK
ME AS AN EGYPTIAN WITH A FEZ AND AN ERECTION

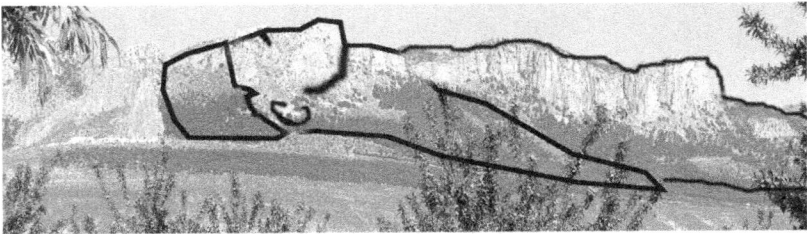

SORRY,I JUST HAVE A VIVID IMAGINATION

Ok That's about the end of the book, but there were quite a lot of personal opinions and oddments that I wanted to include . So this last section is just lots of odds and ends. I want to say thank you to all the people who contributed their own incidents, sorry that I had to leave some out due to repetition or suitability. Hope it all helped to make it a worthwhile read.

View from my cave house window. A lot different than the one from my previous life in Northampton. There all I could see was a row of cars and my neighbours bedroom

ODDS AND ENDS

There is a line of ants that have decided to come up through a small hole in my concrete yard. They march determinedly in a line and disappear down another hole some ten yards away. They have been doing this for days. Having nothing better to do I sat there contemplating this, mug of tea in hand. Why, if they are so good at tunnelling, do they need to come to the surface for such a short distance? Secondly and more puzzling, why are they all going in the same direction, none of them are returning with goodies. They are like a massive Chinese army, there must be billions of them. That is of course unless I am seeing the same ones on subsequent round trips because they have a different hidden return route. A friend suggested I spray a section of them with harmless coloured paint to see if they come round again, seems a bit cruel to me. Don't think I would fancy being sprayed by a giant with a 100 foot aerosol can.

Some jokes about the Spanish, but just to make it fair I have alternated with ones about the British.

How many Spaniards does it take to change a light bulb?

Just Juan

Why do the English make better lovers than the Spanish? Because English are the only ones who can stay on top for 45 minutes and still come second.

One morning, two Brits are strolling down a London street, when they see a stray dog licking its own testicles. One of them turns to the other and says, " I wish I could do that!" His mate watches the dog for a moment, sighs longingly, and replies, "I should say so! But don't you think you ought to get to know him first?"

What do you call a Spaniard whose vehicle was stolen? Carlos!

An American tourist goes into a restaurant in Spain and orders the speciality of the house. When his dinner arrives, he asks the waiter what it is. "These, Senor," replied the waiter in broken English, is the testicles of the bull killed in the ring today." The tourist swallowed hard but tasted the dish and thought it was delicious. So he comes back the next evening and orders the same item. When it is served, he says to the waiter, "These testicles are much smaller than the ones I had last night." "Yes, Senor," replied the waiter, "You see...the bull, he does not always lose.

Butter is mantequilla (meant to kill you)

Why wasn't Jesus born in Spain? He couldn't find 3 wise men or a virgin.

This next one is because Catalans have the reputation in Spain of being cheap, stingy and overworked.

Juan, a respectable business man goes to the local bank and demands to see the manager.

"I am here to solicit a loan, but it must be today."

"It is always a pleasure to be of service, how much do you wish to borrow," says the manager.

"I would like a loan of one euro, to be repaid to you in exactly one month." Says Juan.

"That's too small an amount, I will give it to you from my own pocket," says the manager.

"Absolutely not! You will make out the loan papers correctly. Otherwise I will take all my other business to another bank!" said Juan, "And I will be leaving my Mercedes Benz as collateral."

Fearing to lose a customer who has millions in his account the bank manager agrees.

"Of course, of course, you can leave it in the parking lot right here" says the manager.

Later when Juan sees his wife, he says "Good news, I have found a safe parking place for the Mercedes during our entire month of vacations, for just a euro.

Two Englishmen, two Scotsmen, two Spanish and two Irishmen were marooned on a desert island. The two Scotsmen got together and started a bank; the two Spanish got together and opened a bottle of vino; the two Irishmen got together and started a fight; The two Englishmen never spoke to each other - they hadn't been introduced!

A Spaniard was asked what 'Manana' meant. He explained the term meant. 'Maybe the next day, maybe the day after that. Perhaps next week, next month, next year. Who cares?" An Irishman who was listening butted in and responded. 'In Ireland we don't have a word to describe that degree of urgency.

Time for a moan, this is nothing to do with Spain, just my top ten favourite hates. Got to get the word count up, otherwise it may be a very thin book. These are not in any particular order.

Cooking. Being a male who lives on his own, you either become very good at cooking, or as in my case hate it. If it takes more than fifteen, no ten minutes then I'm not interested. What it the point of spending hours selecting the right ingredients in half a dozen shops, carefully measuring and blending then cooking for half the day, just to shove it all down your throat in a mass, complete with a healthy dose of saliva. Sorry to be distasteful, but the moment it enters your mouth it is all downhill from there. Although I live in the middle of nowhere I have the good fortune to get new neighbours who live just ten minutes away by car. The mother supplemented their income by making ready meals. Now those of you who live in cities and towns are well used to a host of takeaways just within the vicinity, but out here where the nearest Chinese restaurant is more or less fifty miles away or more, they have never heard of a chip shop and there may be a curry house in Granada if you want to hare down the motorway for an hour and a half, after first circumnavigating half an hour of pothole lanes. So suddenly being able to pick up a meal, was bliss, and still is at the time of writing this. Not only that but they don't charge enough; I could not buy the stuff for that. Someone told me that for a portion fish and chips in England you would be paying about seven pounds. And the best bit of this arrangement is I didn't have to peel anything or even put the oven on, just throw the meal in the microwave.

Ironing. I just loath it, what is the point. I know some smart arse is going to say just hang them properly and tug out the creases so that they only need a light ironing. (But that is still ironing) Who invented the ironing board, why can't it be big enough to lay the shirt down without it draping all over the floor, and why can't the board have arms? Why is the cord on the iron always too short and starts twisting on itself? Why does the iron holding tray never hold the iron properly and who in god's name needs to iron underpants and socks. I saw on YouTube a guy who threw a handful of ice cubes into the tumble dryer with some creased dry clothes. Fifteen minutes on moderate heat and all the shirts came out un-creased. Now that's a man after my own heart, pity I don't own a tumble dryer.

Visitors. Don't get me wrong, I have some good friends that I am always pleased to see. But we all have a life to lead and after three days I am champing at the bit to get on with it. Just because I live where it's sunny, doesn't mean I am on vacation and can entertain guests with all the local sights and sounds because they are on holiday.

Entertainment. Yes I use the internet and watch things on YouTube from time to time. But I get to choose and it gets turned off at the end. I hardly watch any films and after twenty minutes, often get bored and turn them off. My beef is with mass entertainment is that most of it is shallow, do I really want to watch people prancing around with stupid grins, Nice to see you, to see you nice!

Smart phones and mobiles in general I saw a group of teenagers outside their local college, a whole row of about twenty, and everyone staring intently at the square of plastic in their hands. Not one of them was attempting any form of conversation with their neighbour. At the airport waiting area, thirty people sitting, and apart from about four who were actually staring into space, they were all on their smart phones. At my dentist last week, everyone was corresponding with the great God internet. I had my notebook and pen and was scribbling this paragraph down; I think they thought I was weird. I am not against progress and I am sure there are plenty of good arguments in favour of smart phones, but please I don't want to live in a world of the walking (or sitting) dead. Ok I now have to come clean, I just purchased a second hand tablet, which now feels like I have turned traitor to my beliefs. There is no way I am going to cart it around. It is purely so I can put my music on it so that when I am playing at a gig it can scroll through telling me the chords I need to play. This saves having a ring binder that always falls on the floor decanting pages in all directions, and usually half way through a song. It does not look very professional when the guitarist is scrambling around on the floor under the drum set trying to retrieve them before the next song starts, then has to be hauled to his feet because his knees are bad.

I have this annoying habit of getting very fidgety when things go on too long. Films should only be forty minutes at most, Dylan droning on for thirty verses, speeches should be five minutes, yes thank you now get off. This book, if you have just read more than three pages, what is wrong with you? Go do something useful. Even anything I like doing such as art or writing has to be done in short bursts of half hour maximum. Then I get a terrible urge to go and do something different, anything, God! Even sweep the floor. As soon as I get stuck into that then I have a short burst of inspiration and can't wait to get back to the keyboard or easel. The sum of all this is that at the end of the day, you know you have been busy but can't actually pin down any real progress with anything. It gets me very frustrated, especially when I see others who seem to achieve so much with what appears to be little effort. Another problem is that I know I could do a better job if I slowed down and approached things in a more considered way, but in my haste to move on to the next problem I dodge things, certainly well enough to function or pass the less discerning eye, but not good enough in reality, and the problem is me, I know it, but can't be bothered to go that extra mile.

Plastic materials. Ever since I had yellow jaundice and glandular fever when at college, and in my delirium melted a plastic spoon into my cuppa soup then drank it, I have had a loathing of plastic. It took two weeks to get the taste out of my mouth. Particularly cutlery and cheap throwaway cups for wine and beer, at parties

Jewellery and carrying things. I can't stand wearing rings, male earrings, necklaces and watches. I have to wear glasses, although I tried contact lenses but they were worse. It may be a form of claustrophobia, I just don't like things hanging, clinging or strapped to me. It's the same with carrying things, my wallet has to be able to fit in a pocket, none of this money belt or man bag nonsense.

Have a feeling I have mentioned this before somewhere, but banging my head, which is something I do quite regularly living in a cave, makes me want to kill something for the next ten seconds. If I am holding something, then it usually gets hurled across the room. If the offending beam is unlucky and I happen to have a hard tool in my hand, then it receives a heavy blow, which then takes me an hour or more to repair. Normally I am quite placid, so it's a bit scary realising that this anger is only just below the surface.

YOU CAN

I have already mentioned my habit of writing notes for my books during any odd moments that I may have, and having to use whatever I can find to write with and on, when out and about. Well I am now waiting for a friend outside the butchers shop, and judging by the numbers waiting and the locals habit of having a long conversation, then he could be in there for some time. So I am writing this on the back page of my car owner's manual, which is shiny paper and the pencil keeps slipping, but it's all I have. Thinking back in the past I have used receipts, toilet paper, pulled out of the shopping bag and not a good idea as the pencil goes though it too easily. The greasy wrapping around meat purchases, my arm with a biro, and even keywords to jog my memory written in the dust on my car window.

If I have absolutely nothing to write with then I have to try and remember my ideas till I get home. That is not easy for someone who forgets almost everything five minutes after hearing it. Trying to remember things has always been difficult for me. When I am stretched out in bed, I get good ideas, or remember things I need to do the next day. If I have been organised and left a pen and pad by the bed, I can reach out even in the dark and scribble a couple of words that will kick start my thoughts the next day. If I have nothing to write with and am too lazy to get up again then I have to get inventive. I will reach out and wrap a discarded sock around my glasses on the bedside desk, or throw one shoe in the far corner, so that the next morning I have to wonder why I did that and with luck then remember the reason. Leaving your car keys in an unusual spot is not a good idea. The next day when you are late and panicking because you can't find them puts everything else out of your mind. So even when at last you stumble across them, remembering your brilliant idea from the night before, is now the last thing on your mind.

Having got this far you may be thinking blimey I could do better than this, perhaps I should write a book. For most people that's how far it gets but for the persistent few it's not so hard as you would imagine.

So you want to write a book? These notes came from a book I wrote about how to write, upload and sell your efforts.

YOU DON'T HAVE TO BE A WRITER TO WRITE

Like a lot of people I always thought that there was a book in me somewhere. I had faithfully filled in my diary each evening and could look at the row of cheap folders in the bookcase. Looking back through them was interesting although what I had for breakfast obviously denoted a rather slack day .It was one particularly boring evening of television when I glanced across at the bookshelf and realized that the volume of words I had scribbled down would easily have produced three sizable novels, had they been about any subject, other than myself. Even then, if I had led a life full of adventure, it would have been OK. As it was I was into my fifteenth year as a school teacher, who would want to read about that? Two weeks later I found my old copy of LUCKY JIM by Kingsley Amis and started re-reading it again. Suddenly I had my second epiphany; here I was reading an amusing fiction story about the education system. I could write one about my exploits or even better still, just use my insider knowledge, create a character that was far more interesting than me and just let my imagination wander.

So if you feel that there is a book in you, then take note of my simple guidelines.

1. Stop doing a Diary about what you ate or watched on television.

2. Grab a pen and fresh notebook or practice your one fingered typing skills, put down everything that could eventually be expanded into an incident. It does not matter if the original event was not that amusing or interesting, artistic license will allow you to improvise, after all it is fiction.

3. Put down any and everything that comes into your head, don't worry about how bad an idea it is or spelling, just go with the flow and brainstorm. Someone recently said, "Write like a maniac" and that is exactly how you should approach it. Don't let negative thoughts get in the way, use short bursts of writing (10 minutes a time) and put down anything that comes from your musings. Don't worry about how it sounds when you read it back, just go with the flow.

Remember, first the ideas, pruning and construction can come later. Write every day, make it a habit, you can set aside time, but if something prevents you then you have lost valuable writing time. I have a pad and pen in my back pocket, I will write whilst the kettle is boiling or even sitting on the loo (sorry about the imagery) but there are plenty of five minute moments when you could easily add a short paragraph or two. Little and often can work better than long stretches at the keyboard.

If you see a pattern emerging in your writing then maybe that is the direction your first book should go in. However it does not matter if you end up with pages of non-linkable ideas, they are all potential starting points. Ask yourself questions, and then answer the question.

4. Finally (It does not matter how long this takes, (never feel guilty or under pressure) When you think you have the basic idea, try and see if you can find ways to split it into twelve sections. If it is a fiction story, have a beginning and an end that takes care of two. Now try to imagine a set of circumstances that can link the two together.

5. Once you have started, ideas will pop into your head at all the wrong moments, so have a pen and note pad handy, by your bed, in the car and a tiny one in your pocket. If you see an interesting article or hear something on the radio, make a note of it.

6. Don't get distracted, little and often is better than full steam ahead than stop for ages. Initial enthusiasm will wane, so get into a habit, which keeps it all going.

7. ENJOY, what is the point of doing something that is a grind.

I like amusing fiction stories, but if your thing is describing toy trains over the last thirty years, then just go for it. The only rule is rule number 7, if it is not fun, then don't do it.

I am now on my eighth e-book and have not run out of ideas for my main character yet. Believe me, once you get into it, there will not be enough hours in the day.

Don't start it by dreaming about being published and making a fortune so that you can give up your day job. If that happens, let me know your secrets, in fact write a book about it and make even more money.

Start because you really would do it, even if you never sold a single copy.

Don't let anyone read your notes, don't ask anyone's opinion, in fact if you can keep your mouth shut, tell nobody anything. Why? Because they will dilute your enthusiasm, make suggestions that confuse your initial ideas and generally put a damper on everything. Just because they can't, or won't do it, they don't want you to either. Criticism is cheap, effort takes time and energy.

MORE BITS

For the first time I have grown marijuana, only two plants and I think you are allowed three by law for personal use. Being a non-smoker meant I have had to think of another way to use them. Somebody told me about green butter, but the thought of swallowing lumps of butter whatever colour makes me feel queasy. I thought about cookies, but having consumed five at a friend's house without any reaction, I decided that some form of alcohol should do the trick. So for the last three weeks the leaves and stems (not the seeds, they will blow your head off) have been marinating in a bottle of cheap vodka. Next week will be the test, some orange or tonic and a couple of ice cubes and settle myself on the terrace. I will report back.

Those of you who read the first Grumpy book will remember my loathing for house cleaning and general chores and the different games I created just to make myself do the bare minimum. Well Eureka! I've seen the light, been converted, am a New Age man now. It came to me in a blinding flash, a message from some higher being, that if I wanted to keep friends and influence people into believing that I was clean, tidy, organized or even capable (God! I hate those words) then I would have to swallow the pill and just waste large portions of my week, broom in hand. No change of faith comes without a struggle and sacrifice, but now my floor has seen the light, so I may as well follow its example. I tell you what, assigning two hours a day to washing and cleaning is far harder for me than it ever was to go from 40 cigarettes a day to giving it all up.

Just been to make a coffee, stuck my head into my bedroom because one of the dogs seem to be missing. He had snuck in there pulled my pillow off the bed ripped it to bits and was sitting innocently in a giant pile of yellow foam chunks. Obviously I have not explained my new intentions clearly enough to him.

Time for some more moaning

This will also be the last time I air my own personal feelings in print, so excuse me if I leave the humour behind and finish on a more serious note.

I can't help being a dinosaur, it's just in my nature to resist the advance of technology, it took me five years to allow a CD to enter my home, it was always vinyl for me. No doubt if I had been born earlier, I would have been jealously guarding my phonograph or unless you played the lute or dulcimer you would not be allowed in the house with an electric guitar. It was the same when I stated writing as a hobby, it was always the trusty typewriter, and the computer and its devil child 'Word' were not to be trusted. Oh well! Everything changes, and so do I, but only after a bit of kicking and screaming. Being a 'dino' has some advantages, you don't rush into spending your hard earned money on the next bright shiny object, something you don't actually need, but suddenly it becomes indispensable. It shows how far behind I am only recently considered buying a blender, because I have put my dogs on a diet consisting of a lot more natural veg. The shop wanted 45 euro for this thing, which could reduce my beans and carrots to mush. As I can do a decent job with a sharp knife in five minutes I declined. We can waste two and a half hours watching a crap film we know we should turn off, but need a blender to save us a few minutes ! Try chopping it's good for controlling aggression, but possibly not for your fingers, Ha!

Fake plastic world

Not having had a TV for over 12 years, it came as quite a shock to me when friends rigged me up with one whilst recovering from my latest operation. I really appreciate their kind thought and it did take my mind off the pain when I could not concentrate on my hobbies, but unfortunately I really am not a television addict. I remember reading sometime in the past that if you kept the population mindlessly entertained for long periods, then you would have far less problems controlling them. I forced myself to sit through banal drivel that I have heard people say is excellent such as, 'I'm a nobody get me out of here,' or 'Come dancing, I only did five years at stage school'. Also 'I'm a star on X Factor for five minutes' but will spend the next thirty years singing in dingy working men's clubs on the basis of being on telly once. Actually I felt sorry for the singers, some of them were better than most of the judges. These programmes are pure plastic world drivel, for mass consumption. Then there is Jeremy Kyle. So what if one pair of morons have been doing something to another pair of morons, who are then willing to go on TV to expose their grubby little secrets for five minutes of fame. Even sport! It takes five grown men forty minutes, with endless slow motion re runs to discuss how somebody managed to prod a ball into a net at one end of a field.

We buy, we consume and we discard as soon as something newer becomes available. Consumerism has taken over the world; it has nothing to do with actually needing things. In the past it was only missionaries and monks who dedicated themselves to a life of calling. Now even salesmen are doing it.

"My CRUSADE is to identify what someone would want to buy after they have had an intense experience." Head of Sales, Tate Gallery.

The mind boggles.

I watched a fashion parade on TV, some of the male models came out wearing ballet skirts, suspenders holding up men's socks and on their heads they had flowery hats that looked like they had been retrieved from a windy day at Ascot. "Give me strength"

I changed channels and watched David Attenborough drone on for an hour about the life cycle of newts. Actually that was more interesting than most stuff on TV and at least he didn't go to stage school.

I always thought it would be good to have a pause button in life, so that when things got too much you could press it and to all intense and purposes just disappear for a length of time. You would be in stasis; no pressure of daily life then when you had time to recover could bring yourself back in at the moment you left but with the knowledge of having had a good rest. I suppose that's what having your body cryogenically frozen is almost about, although I think they need a bit more work on that before I would trust it. I often think that some animals have it better sussed than us, especially the ones that hibernate. If we humans did that just think of the saving on the worlds resources.

Some people have the knack of making money, whilst the majority struggle. Most of us lie somewhere in between. I have never understood why no matter what I earn or don't earn, I am still always on the negative side of my finances. I suppose that the logic of it is that subconsciously we spend according to our needs. But even when I experimented by spending virtually nothing on myself for two months I still came out on minus figures. You get very frustrated when you come out of the supermarket with just the bare essentials and no treats. It was the same in England when I had a regular job. I would love to stack my supermarket trolley high, just once. I have never had to support a large family, how the hell do they manage it?

Credit is so readily available; you can borrow £10,000 without any viable income to support repayments. I have refused loans that were almost pressed on me by the bank. I know it is quite easy to live on negative figures, I've had a lot of practice, but it always leaves a hollow feeling in your stomach. Money may not be able to make you happy, but it does relieve some of the tension and ease the palpitations when the statements arrive on your mat. I know its only numbers; I keep telling myself that I have a home, car and enough for food, which is far better than billions of people have. I should count myself very lucky, but it's natural to look at the world from one's own situation.

In today's world it is very easy to feel sorry for oneself. The people who struggle most are the ones who can't accept the incessant unfairness of life. They become consumed with what should have happened that they become incapable of dealing with reality.

Self-pity is the refuge of the weak (but I like being weak sometimes) what fat lard arse advertising executive came up with the slogan 'What does not kill you makes you stronger' obviously he hasn't just had to replace a car tyre, using a wonky jack at seven in the morning, when my already ruined knees and shoulder that really don't like the cold, are giving me grief. Mind you when I think life is tough, try being a fly on a sticky tape catcher. (This is after watching, them whilst I made tea.)

You may be weak, boring, timid, overweight, and obnoxious or any of a thousand other afflictions, but as long as you don't know it, then life is good.

"Without stress life would be empty."

Live the life you have now, in the time frame you are in and try and enjoy it, even if I can't, Ha!

Time is very precious, and the older you get the more you value it and seek to use it more wisely. Time wasted can never be saved.

In previous years my life drifted on, with a backdrop of work and in a country and language that I understood. It was safe and when looked at as a whole, very boring. I assumed I would get older, retire, potter around then pass on to whatever. That is still going to happen, but somehow it is different now.

I'm not a pessimist, I like to think of myself more as a realist, why hide from the inevitable. Let's face it, getting old is not much fun. For years you put it off, by convincing yourself that whatever stage you are passing through, is nowhere near the end one. Even when people start offering to carry your bags or get up and usher you into their seat, realisation does not dawn and you mutter under your breath that their help is not necessary. Another sign is when you start reading about Saga holidays in the magazine in the doctor's waiting room. If you actually go ahead and book one, then you have at least subconsciously accepted the fact, even if you won't admit it. Hot Cocoa and in bed by 10pm, is also a sign. Especially if you have declined an invitation to a good party. By the time the truth hits you, it can be quite a bummer. Nothing is going to get better, healthier or easier, no matter how many sit ups you can still do. Additional cosmetic war paint and God forbid plastic surgery, it hides nothing and if anything accentuates the desperation of warding off time. Pills are no longer singular but form a neat row on the medicine cabinet shelf. Or,may even require being distributed in a sectioned box, with numbered days in big letters.

We push the days ahead to the back of our mind. I am now realising that I have been in Spain longer, than I am likely to survive. Death does not scare me as long as it's quick and hopefully painless. But as most of us have to go through the dribbling stage, possibly at both ends, unless something more virulent gets us, it does bring up the consideration of jumping off the nearest high mountain. Trouble is by the time I realise it's definitely time to check out, I will probably be incapable of walking up there, or of even knowing which direction the mountain is in.

This next paragraph was lifted out of Quora (If you don't know that website look it up, it's very interesting, people ask all sorts of questions and usually the answers are good) So I can't credit who said it, but I am sure they won't mind. It was told by a 90 year old woman when asked what it was like to be old.

When you're about 25 or so.... you are pretty much who you are and will always be on the inside. With time, you may fluctuate in some beliefs or improve or not improve yourself in small bits. If you're wise, you learn as much as you can. But you are pretty much you. You experience life - maybe marriage, kids, travel, loss, joy. You start understanding the perspectives of your parents, your children. At about 35, you start to feel and look a little different, older. By 40, you start to really feel physical changes but depending upon how you took care of yourself, they might be bad or not. At 50, you look decidedly different in face and body although some age better than others. At 60, nobody is all that pleased with their physical state. That is why it is IMPERATIVE that you work on your inside. That you develop self-love, that is deeper than surface appearances. That you do your best to live without regrets.

"The regret for things we've done can be tempered with time but regrets for those things we did not do, those are inconsolable."

When the old lady woke up... at first, she felt 25 again. Then she turned her head to look at the clock and her neck told her she was at least 35. Then she moved an arm and was 45. Then a leg and was 55. Then sat up and was 65. Then stood up and was 75. She then started walking toward her bathroom and was 85... and then she turned to face the mirror and thought,

""Who the fuck is that?"

Anyway this book is now finished and it will be time to move on to other projects. Thank you for reading it, sorry if you are annoyed or don't agree about anything mentioned in these pages. My intention was not to offend. Anyway there is nothing stopping you putting pen to paper and writing your own book.

There definitely won't be an 'Even more Grumpy in Spain book'.

MY OTHER BOOKS

GRUMPY IN SPAIN

Humorous personal experiences and opinions about my new adopted country. The differences of attitude between two European neighbours.

MORE GRUMPY IN SPAIN

My present book follows on from, 'Grumpy in Spain'. Having run out of my own adventures it is mostly a collection of opinions, information and funny articles from others.

THE COLLECTOR OF LIFE

Written under a pen name (KIM ORSON) it is a fiction science fantasy about coming back from the dead, and getting a job. Although the humour is somewhat dark, it is not as depressing as the title may suggest.

SERIES OF SHORT STORIES

Each book has a theme.

THE BARGE Slightly dark tales.

THE PAINTER Tales with warm endings.

DOG STORIES AND HAIRY TALES Yep! All about dogs.

There will be more in this series.

THE ART OF STUPIDITY

Originally three separate books, it is now a compilation. The hilarious antics of a teacher, his pupils, friends and enemies, spread over a host of calamitous events.

WRITE, UPLOAD, SELL

Have you ever wanted to write a book and get it published? This instructional book will definitely get you over the hurdles.

FORTHCOMING PROJECTS

THE ARTIST DAY BOOK   (Provisional title)

Having taught adults in art lessons for several years, I compiled loads of notes and ideas for them. These are being arranged and will appear as a kind of lesson a week for anyone wanting to take up art as a hobby. (Release date aimed for late 2018)

SKETCHES OF ANDALUCIA   (Provisional title)

I have drawn numerous sketches of sites around this part of Spain, most took only about ten minutes each, as I am not keen on people wandering up to watch. My motto is get in, record and get out. The intention is to compile them into a book. This should be available by late-2018.

PRIVATE THOUGHTS AND DESIRES (Provisional title)

My attempt at a saucy fiction book. May take quite a while, my imagination has its limits in this category. Started as a challenge from a friend. I got rather embarrassed writing some bits, wondering where my dirty imagination came from. Not sure I will get around to publishing it, unless it's under a different name.

GETTING THROUGH THE DAY

Kind of self-help manual, on hold till revisions undertaken. This developed out of trying to heal myself, I don't claim to be an authority, but it helped to work out some of my issues, so it may be of some use to others who suffer from similar maladies.

ABOUT THE AUTHOR

John Moody came to Spain in a last ditch attempt to create a fresh new life, seeing as how the old one had grown stale. The experiment actually worked and since then he has led a far more active and interesting life. (Hey who said?) Well actually it's true. I have not made many correct decisions in my life, but coming over here was one of the few inspired ones. At times I get down and grumpy, but never lose the appreciation of having found another vibrant and interesting life style.

PICTURE IS SCARY I KNOW

24397434R00098

Made in the USA
Columbia, SC
27 August 2018